*How to support
and teach*
children on the
autism spectrum

Dave Sherratt

Dedication

To all children on the autism spectrum, in every corner of the world.

Acknowledgements

Ideas are rarely developed in isolation, and the ones in this book are no exception. This work has been inspired by children in North Yorkshire schools and by the teaching of Gill Donald, Jane Gibb and Debbie Patrick, who work in the Social-Communication Resource at Mowbray School. Furthermore, the theoretical underpinnings of the book are based on Sherratt and Peter (2002) and Sherratt and Donald (2004). I should therefore like to thank the staff, governors, volunteers, children and families at Mowbray School, as well as my co-authors, for their contributions. I am indebted to you all.

I owe a debt of thanks to Professor Rita Jordan and Professor Jill Boucher; Dr Melanie Peter and Dr Yiannis Vogindroukas; the staff and students at the University of Birmingham; and my friends and colleagues from around the world, especially in India, Greece and the United States, who have helped to shape the ideas. I am also grateful to Cathy Griffin, Debbie Pullinger, Rebecca Barnes, and the editorial team at LDA, all of whom made valuable contributions to the finished work.

A final word of thanks to my children Heidi, Jack and Grace, who have allowed me the time to study and to write, and who have tolerated my special interest in autism.

Permission to photocopy

This book contains materials which may be reproduced by photocopier or other means for use by the purchaser. This permission is granted on the understanding that these copies will be used within the educational establishment of the purchaser. This book and all its contents remain copyright. Copies may be made without reference to the publisher or to the licensing scheme for the making of photocopies operated by the Publishers' Licensing Agency.

The right of Dave Sherratt to be identified as author of this work has been asserted by him in accordance with sections 77 and 78 of the Copyright, Designs and Patents Act 1988.

How to support and teach children on the autism spectrum
MT01151
ISBN-13: 978 1 85503 390 0

Printed in the UK for LDA
Abbeygate House, East Road, Cambridge, CB1 1DB, UK

Contents

Contents

Introduction

Autism is a difference in thinking style. Children who have an autistic thinking style see the world in a different way from the majority of other children. This means that their behaviour sometimes seems odd and difficult to understand. It also means that they will learn about the world in a different way.

Children with this thinking style can be found throughout the educational system and in every type of school. Most schools will have at least one child on the autism spectrum, and large schools may have several children at any one time.

Children who have learning needs on the autism spectrum require an appropriate education that will help them understand and function effectively in the world in which we all live, that will encourage their need to engage and communicate with others, and that respects the culture in which they live. They may receive this education in mainstream or independent schools, in schools for gifted children or in the many other types of special school that exist.

Teachers, parents and all who work with children on the autism spectrum need strategies that will help them deliver this education and support their development. This book has been written to provide those working with these children with a range of strategies and activities to help them in their endeavour. All the strategies suggested have come out of real-life classroom practice with children on the autism spectrum.

Who will benefit from this book?

This book is primarily for class teachers, SENCos and teaching assistants who work with children in the primary age range who are on the autistic spectrum. It may also be of interest to headteachers, therapists, psychologists, parents, and anyone else who is involved in the education of children with autism, Asperger syndrome or another autism spectrum condition.

Chapter 1
What does it mean to be on the autism spectrum?

Read the dialogue opposite and picture the scene. A shopper has gone into a cosy café for some refreshment. They approach the counter . . .

It's an unremarkable scene. The action is what we might call normal social behaviour and there is a shared narrative amongst the characters. Now turn the page, and imagine a similar scene with a slightly different dialogue.

The behaviour of the characters in this second scene will probably strike you as odd. The café owner mysteriously winks twice before speaking and seems determined to sell the apple tart and milk, rather than satisfy the customer. Customer 1 is very polite and wants to talk about the weather. Customer 2 is only saying what they really think, and does not make polite conversation. Having been disappointed by the apple tart, they have no qualms about suggesting they have some of the other customer's cake.

These characters are not meant to be autistic, but they may give you some idea of what it feels like when each person brings a different narrative to the plot. It is as if each person is an actor who has a different script. Each has a valid script, but they do not make sense when put together. To have autism or to be on the autism spectrum is not to engage fully or intuitively with the social narrative.

What is autism?

The second café scene may give you a sense of the lack of shared understanding that characterises communication with someone on the autism spectrum. It is not like speaking to someone who doesn't speak your language, when you can simply communicate without words because you have shared expectations and understanding of human behaviour. It is more like meeting someone who does not speak your language well, and whose anger or anxiety is making them highly unpredictable. Their language, actions and expressions do not mesh with your understanding, and your responses are consequently insensitive, poorly timed and sometimes simply the wrong thing to say.

With time, it is possible for both parties to find patterns in each other's behaviour and to develop a shared understanding of typical situations and interactions, but this social problem-solving is mentally demanding and difficult to manage when other demands are being made at the same time. Children with autism sometimes attempt to use this type of processing to make sense of the world around them, but many find it laborious, and so display a range of disengaged behaviours that others find it difficult to make sense of.

"On no account may you sit in this conspicuously empty seat."

Tea and cake 1

1

Customer 1:	A cup of tea and a slice of chocolate cake, please.
Café owner:	*(smiling)* Certainly, would you like milk and sugar in your tea?
Customer 1:	Milk, but no sugar, thank you.
Café owner:	There you are. Which of the chocolate cakes would you like?
Customer 1:	A slice of that one, please.
Café owner:	Of course. Anything else?
Customer 1:	No, thanks. How much is that?
Café owner:	That'll be £2.50 altogether. Thank you. And here's your change.

Finding all tables are occupied, the customer decides to try to join another customer who has a spare seat at their table.

Customer 1:	Excuse me, is anyone sitting here? Would you mind if I had this seat?
Customer 2:	Not at all. Let me move my newspaper. Did you get caught in the rain just now?
Customer 1:	Yes, I thought I'd come in here and dry off a bit. Did you get wet as well?
Customer 2:	No, I came in before it started. Do you like that chocolate cake? I had a slice and thought it was very nice.
Customer 1:	Mmmm. I'm very partial to chocolate cake – and this one is delicious!

Tea and cake 2

2

Customer 1: A cup of tea and a slice of chocolate cake, please.

Café owner: (*winking twice*) Oh, I don't think so . . . not today. Would you like milk instead? It is very white.

Customer 1: No, I don't like milk, thank you. Do you have any tea?

Café owner: (*winking twice*) Yes, of course we have tea, but the milk is very cold and it is also very white. Why don't you have the milk instead?

Customer 1: Er . . . no, thank you. But I will have a slice of chocolate cake, please.

Café owner: Hmm . . . (*winking twice*) the chocolate cakes are delicious. Which apple tart would you like?

Customer 1: Could I have a slice of that chocolate cake, please?

Café owner: (*winking twice*) Of course. Would you like cream on the apple tart?

Customer 1: No, thank you! I would like a cup of tea and a slice of chocolate cake . . . please.

Customer 1: (*winking twice*) Well . . . it is against my better judgement to let customers have what they want, but if you insist . . . that will be £2.50. Thank you. I may give you your change later, if you decide you would like the apple tart as well.

Finding all tables are occupied, the customer decides to try to join another customer who has a spare seat at their table.

Customer 1: Excuse me, is anyone sitting here? Would you mind if I had this seat?

Customer 2: On no account may you sit in this conspicuously empty seat next to me. You look like an unsavoury character and you will probably drip rainwater onto my clean table. I wish you would sit on the floor instead.

Customer 1: Thank you, you are most obliging. You are quite right, I did get caught out in the rain, but I am most grateful for the kind hospitality and warm welcome that I have received in this establishment.

Customer 2: I wish you would go away and not bother me with your meaningless chatter. If you don't go soon, I might have to take a bite out of your chocolate cake.

Customer 1: The weather is truly awful outside. Have you seen a recent weather forecast? It looks as if it might rain for some time.

Customer 2: This apple tart is not nice. If I sit on the floor instead, would you let me have some of your cake?

Autism and autism spectrum conditions can therefore be described as difficulties in engaging in a shared narrative. They consist of a different thinking style.

'Autism is not a single condition but a collection of conditions that have common behavioural characteristics.'

Children who have an autistic thinking style typically see the world in a different way from the majority of other children. This means that their behaviour is sometimes odd and difficult to understand. It also means that they will learn about the world in a different way, and their understanding lacks a shared and common foundation for learning from and with others.

Scientists are still unsure about the physiological basis of autism. Its cause is probably partly genetic, and it may be affected by environmental factors, such as diet. The important thing to realise, however, is that it is not a single condition but a collection of conditions that have common behavioural characteristics. These vary in severity, and one person's symptoms may change over time and with development.

Areas of difficulty

Autism can affect people across a wide range of intellectual abilities and skills. All children on the autism spectrum will have difficulty in some areas of social understanding, and this can manifest itself in a variety of ways, including:

- an apparent uninterest in other people;
- subtle difficulties in understanding what other people really think, especially when they have said something open to interpretation;
- difficulties in communicating thoughts and feelings – this is evidenced in a range of ways, from the frustration of children who want something but do not think to tell anyone about it, to the problems of those who would like to make friends but who always seem to say the wrong thing;
- some inflexibility in thinking or behaviour – they may insist on sticking with familiar routines, such as always walking to school by the same route, or they may develop special and sometimes unusual interests that absorb them for hours at a time, such as an interest in maps that show the route to school;
- unusual interests, or fascination with the perceptual properties of objects or with abstract ideas such as time;
- difficulty in finding connections and drawing them together into a relevant thread or social narrative.

Identification

The essential features for a clinical diagnosis of autism or Asperger syndrome are given by the World Health Organisation and the American Psychiatric Association. These criteria are used by psychiatrists, psychologists, paediatricians and others who work in multidisciplinary diagnostic teams. Children who would benefit from a formal assessment or diagnosis of autism should be referred to a specialist autism team. However, help can often be provided by experienced colleagues working in teaching, psychology, psychiatry, paediatrics or speech and language therapy.

Opposite is a checklist of behaviours that are typical of children across the autism spectrum. Whilst it does not provide a clinical diagnosis, it may help you in deciding whether to seek further advice about a child who is causing concern. As a very rough guide, seven or more ticks indicate a need to consider referral to a psychologist or other colleague experienced in autism.

Terminology

A wide variety of labels and terms have been applied to children on the autism spectrum.

Autism

Autism has been defined as a developmental difficulty that combines:

○ impairments in or unusual development of social understanding;

○ impairments in or unusual development of communication;

○ a rigidity of thought and action.

This 'triad of impairments' (Wing 1996) is found in all children on the autistic spectrum. In the case of autism, these difficulties are often severe and associated with learning difficulties.

Asperger syndrome

Asperger syndrome is characterised by the same triad of impairments as autism, but without significant learning or structural language difficulties. Features of autism are often more subtle in children with Asperger syndrome, although their effects may be equally severe. Clumsiness is associated with the condition. For educational purposes, it is best to consider autism and Asperger syndrome as being on the same continuum. The educational implications are similar wherever on the spectrum the child is found, as the core difficulties are much the same.

Other conditions

There are many other conditions that are sometimes associated with autism, including semantic-pragmatic language disorder, attention-deficit hyperactivity disorder, Landau-Kleffner syndrome, Rett syndrome, pervasive developmental disorder, fragile-X syndrome, obsessive-compulsive disorder, Tourette syndrome, childhood disintegrative disorder, non-verbal learning disorder and pathological demand avoidance. Whilst some of these conditions are more strongly associated with autism than others, children who have these conditions may also be described as being on the autism spectrum if they have pronounced development delays in social understanding and communication, and have a rigidity of thought and action. The spectrum may also include many children who are described as having severe social and communication difficulties.

Because the situation is far from straightforward, it can be helpful to refer to a child as 'being on the spectrum of autistic conditions', 'having an autism spectrum disorder' or, more simply, as 'being on the autism spectrum'.

Behaviours typical of children across the autism spectrum

Observed behaviour

Uses eyes to communicate in an unusual way	
Does not show an interest in what others are looking at	
Shows a lack of facial expression, or expressions are out of context	
Apparently not interested in others	
Attends to others too intensely	
Stands too close or too far away	
Has few friends and has difficulty in maintaining friendships	
Prefers to be on the outside of social groups	
Likes games to be organised using either consistent rules or those of their own making	
Tends not to share interests with others, or not to point things out or comment on the same topics as normally developing children	
Offers explanations for their behaviour that show little regard for the needs or interests of others	
Rarely comforts or reassures others when they are distressed	
Finds difficulty in working collaboratively with other children	
Tends not to imitate other children or to pick up the subtleties of peer culture	
Appears older than their real age, owing to an adult manner	
Fails to understand things in the same way as other children	
Speaks in an unusually loud or unusually quiet voice	
Has difficulty adapting behaviour to different audiences; they may use the same manner with their teacher as with peers in the playground	

Behaviour	
Has a sense of humour, but doesn't always share this with others; finds difficulty in understanding other people's humour	
Has difficulty in 'reading between the lines' and understanding inferences	
Gives unlikely reasons for the behaviour of other people	
Has difficulties in planning ahead	
Does not treat other people's feelings or points of view as relevant	
Tends to talk at length about a topic of interest	
Has an over-riding interest in an unusual subject, object or person	
Repeats actions, such as foot-tapping in class, inappropriately	
Develops repetitive behaviour patterns such as insisting that they always follow the same route to school	
Knowingly repeats disruptive behaviour such as flicking lights on and off	
Has difficulty in remembering what to do when the context changes	
Has difficulty in getting organised for different lessons	
Becomes anxious when there are unexpected minor changes to the day	
Is not motivated (or perturbed) in the same way as the other children	
Sometimes appears very happy or upset for no apparent reason	
Has an unusually strong reaction if anyone touches them	
Has an unusually strong reaction, such as covering their ears, if someone says a particular word	
Sometimes fails to distinguish between group and individual requests	
Uses particularly clumsy or insensitive attempts to make friends	

Whichever term is used, it is important to see the child as an individual who has a range of aptitudes and skills and who can be described in a variety of ways. For this reason, many people prefer phrases such as 'child with autism' or 'child with an autism spectrum condition', because they put the focus on the child rather than the condition.

In this book, these terms are used interchangeably to mean a group of children across a wide range of abilities, all of whom have difficulties in understanding other people and communicating with them, and who have some rigidity in behaviour or thought.

Using this book

We begin in Chapter 2 by considering the context for the education of children on the autism spectrum.

In Chapters 3 to 5, you will find strategies and activities to help you support and teach the child on the autism spectrum. The main aim throughout is to diminish mutual disengagement and increase opportunities for engagement in shared narrative. The ideas are grouped according to stage of development. For a child at any given developmental level, there are ideas that will be ideally suited, some that are not suitable and others that may be used, providing the objectives of that activity are suitably modified.

Some of the activities will be suitable only for those children who understand their imaginary nature. If you have any doubt about the appropriateness of an activity or the ability of a child to understand pretence, then choose a different activity that is developmentally appropriate. It is not necessarily a problem to use pretence before the child has demonstrated their own understanding of it. Play-drama activities can be used successfully with children with severe autism and severe developmental delay.

The strategies and activities are aimed at children across the spectrum from ages 3 to 11 years, although many can be adapted easily for an older age group. The content of most activities can usually be adapted very easily to suit a particular child or children.

Chapter 6 looks at long- and short-term planning for the child and offers some strategies and ideas for supporting them within the classroom and school environment.

Finally, an important element in the teaching of a child on the autism spectrum is the support given to everyone involved with that child, and this is the focus of the last chapter.

Short answers to some big questions about children on the autism spectrum

Is there a cure?

Although people are searching for a cure, one has not yet been found.

Does a special diet help?

Many children on the autism spectrum are put on a special diet (commonly gluten-free, casein-free or additive-free) in the hope that it will alleviate the symptoms. This seems to make an improvement in some children but not in others. Research is being done to find out why this is.

Do children on the autism spectrum have friends?

Some children on the autism spectrum do have meaningful, long-term relationships. Some, when they grow up, even marry and become good parents. Others find it very difficult to maintain any sort of friendship, even though they would like to. There are also some – particularly those who have more severe forms of autism – who have little interest in other people as friends. The majority of people with autism do have meaningful and valuable relationships with others. The way they express this, however, may be unconventional and may be recognised and understood only by people who know them well.

Are they good at mathematics?

Some children on the autism spectrum develop particular skills and abilities that are exceptional – and these may include mathematical ability. Many children do not have any noticeably exceptional ability, but may nevertheless spend a lot of time on special interests that become highly developed.

Why, when they appear to have understood, do they do the opposite to what I have asked?

Many children on the autism spectrum understand the literal meanings of words but often fail to grasp the subtle meanings that underlie them; they cannot 'read between the lines'. Others do not understand the context or the narrative sequence in which the words are used, and are likely to follow their own thoughts rather than ones that are shared with others.

There are other children in my class who sometimes behave as if they have autism. Is there an increase in the number of children on the autism spectrum?

There is certainly much greater awareness of autism and autism spectrum conditions. This may mean that we are now more likely to interpret the behaviour of some children in terms of autism. It is also possible that there is a genuine increase in the number of children who have autism. However, it is important to recognise that much of the behaviour that characterises autism is seen in all children; it is simply pronounced and extended in children on the autism spectrum.

Children on the autism spectrum are not imaginative or creative, are they?

Many children on the autism spectrum are highly creative and imaginative. They may display this in unusual ways, and they may need prompting to use it in conventional forms. Developing creativity is an important aspect of teaching children on the autism spectrum. (See Chapter 6.)

What can you expect them to achieve educationally?

Children on the autism spectrum have a very wide range of needs and capabilities. Some go on to university; others need long-term care in special communities. It is important not to underestimate the capabilities of any child on the autism spectrum just because they do not demonstrate a particular aptitude at a certain time. Planning should always be for the whole child, taking into account observations, tests, and discussions with parents and other professionals. The school should then devise opportunities for the child to learn about the social and physical aspects of the world so that they can learn to function well within it. Where possible, use professionals experienced in teaching and working with children on the autistic spectrum to help plan both the long- and short-term goals for education and independence.

Chapter 2
Teaching children on the autism spectrum

Where should children on the autism spectrum learn?

Children on the autism spectrum have a very wide variety of educational needs. It is important to determine where these needs will best be met – and this will be different for each child and will vary over time.

Specialised educational provision may supply the knowledge, experience and environments that are essential for some; others gain tremendously from being educated with their peers in an integrated setting. Ideally, each school, unit or class should provide a suitable package based on the needs of each individual, whether in a mainstream or special setting.

Food for thought
Children on the autism spectrum need an education that is designed to meet their specific needs. They need teachers with commitment and enthusiasm who can develop effective relationships and engage meaningfully with them. In this way, they are no different from any other children.

Opposite is a checklist of questions to ask when assessing and evaluating the quality of education offered in a particular school, or the learning environment in a particular class. After working through the questions, talk the answers over with a colleague to decide whether the child's needs are being met.

Which approach works best?

Across the world, there are a number of educational approaches that have been developed or modified specifically for children on the autism spectrum. Most of these are promoted passionately by their advocates, some of whom make remarkable claims. Some approaches offer cure or rapid progress, often citing scientific evidence in support of their methods. Parents and professionals should treat all specialist approaches and educational opportunities with caution, making informed assessments based on their understanding of their child's needs. Useful advice on the types of programme available and the questions that should be asked of these are provided by Jones (2002) and DfES (2002).

Nevertheless, many of these programmes have real value that can easily be lost in the confusion over philosophical or theoretical issues and ethical or financial considerations. Underlying most of these approaches are a number of common fundamental principles that make for successful teaching for children on the autism spectrum. These include:

○ intensive, structured and purposeful teaching;

○ clear, unambiguous and explicit instructions and teaching strategies;

○ use of repetition to consolidate;

Food for thought
Teaching a child on the autism spectrum can be very unsettling and make you feel that you cannot meet the child's needs. Most good teachers feel this at times. Use this uncomfortable feeling as a reason to find out more and explore new ways of teaching.

Quality of education checklist

Do all staff have some understanding of autism and the autism spectrum?	
How do you teach children with autism spectrum conditions to understand their own thoughts and feelings and those of others?	
Do you have strategies for teaching children to communicate?	
Have you assessed the child's needs in all areas of school? Have you discussed this information with staff throughout the school?	
Can the child understand what you want them to do and when? How do you signal a change in routine to the child?	
What strategies do you have for when the child becomes upset, anxious, excitable or angry?	
How do you encourage others to engage and interact with the child?	
Which strategies do you use when the child does not want to do something?	
How do you check that the child has understood and can apply their learning?	
Are your strategies for teaching creativity successful?	
Do you successfully encourage the children to play together?	
How do you help the child to develop their strengths?	
Do parents and professionals have time to liaise?	
Do you have opportunities to discuss difficult issues with a specialist in autism?	
Do you have a supportive friend or colleague with whom to share the problems and joys of teaching children on the autism spectrum?	
How much time during the day is the child engaged with their work / engaged with other people / not engaged with productive learning / engaged with their own thoughts and feelings? Given the child's learning needs, does this profile offer an effective use of their time?	

Permission to Photocopy

- re-teaching in different contexts and in different ways, not assuming that the child has understood because they have repeated or demonstrated something;

- the use of a communicative form that the child understands and can use to convey ideas to others (for many children, visual methods are the most effective; others manage speaking and listening well, while others need to base their learning on their experience of the world);

- opportunities for learning with a personal meaning that is interesting and motivating;

- a high level of adult tuition and support;

- the development of meaningful relationships with others.

Meeting the child's needs

It is easy to over-estimate the abilities of children on the autistic spectrum. A child who enjoys answering subtraction and multiplication questions and is reading from Shakespeare at 7 years old may have a social-communicative developmental age of 18 months. Reading and mathematics may not be a priority for this child. Instead they need to develop a shared understanding of the world; to see it as others see it. To do this, the child needs to establish mental connections with others about ideas, feelings, attitudes, opinions and beliefs as well as about objects and events. They also need to learn in an environment where they feel that other children and adults understand and care for them, and for at least some of the time see the world as they see it. In this supportive environment, the child can make connections with others and learn to see the world in a different and interconnected way.

"That which we call a rose by any other name would smell as sweet"

Food for thought
Autism is an adventure. We share a journey together and explore different ways of understanding the world. It is our responsibility to make this adventure a positive and enjoyable one.

A whole-school approach

Whether the setting is a special school or mainstream education, a whole-school approach is vital. All staff need to have some understanding of the child's condition and needs. Policies should be written and discussed to assist staff in understanding the child's behaviour and responding appropriately, whether in the classroom, at playtime, at lunchtime or at home time. See Chapter 7 for some ideas for support and training.

Child safety and protection

As I arrived at school yesterday, the children in a primary autism class were at play. One teacher and two children were spinning on the spot being helicopters, a child was giggling excitedly as a teacher was waiting for him at the bottom of the slide pretending to be some kind of monster, another child had grazed his knee from falling over and was seeking comfort by hugging a teacher, and two children were shrieking with laughter as they played a game of chase around the trunk of an old tree.

In that physical play session, the children were meaningfully engaged, making communicative use of eye contact and using gesture and speech to direct others and share their excitement. Many children on the autism spectrum only allow meaningful relationships to develop when they are engaged in such activities.

Many of the strategies and activities in this book are 'techniques of affective engagement' that use physical contact. As such, they require special consideration of matters of safety, respect and wellbeing. Where possible, child protection policies should be agreed in advance. The following points should be considered:

- The aim must be for all adults and children to develop high levels of trust in each other. Professionals who use physical contact as part of an activity should not enter into it without explaining its goals, parameters and child-safety issues with parents and colleagues. Children also need to understand what is happening. Children who do not understand speech sufficiently should be carefully introduced to any activity in small steps. Professionals working in this way should be transparent in their practice and overseen by others, so that misunderstandings do not arise.

- Physical contact is acceptable only for certain areas of the body, namely the arms, hands, shoulders, head and feet. Areas such as the neck, back, tummy, and legs below the knee may be used in some circumstances, with an increased level of caution. No other area of the body should be used in play. Children should be treated with care and respect at all times.

- There may be cultural reasons to limit the areas of the body used; if so, these rules must be agreed with all who work with the child. Consideration should also be given to the age of the child. High levels of physical contact may not be appropriate with older children unless the long- and short-term implications have been thoroughly thought out, discussed and documented. However, there are sometimes good reasons to continue with this type of play into adulthood.

- Ensure that you provide a safe environment and sufficient protection for children if they fall over or attempt to climb on furniture. This is particularly important in games that involve high levels of physical contact, such as rough-and-tumble play.

- Some children will already have established fears about objects and events that have no adverse effects on others. These are sometimes difficult to predict, but may be associated with times of high emotion and confusion such as birthday parties. Other children may display great anxiety when confronted with everyday objects such as balloons or cameras. It is important to find out as much as possible about the likes and dislikes of each child, and to proceed with some caution when using highly affective teaching techniques (e.g. Spider in the Box in Chapter 5). See the Interest checklist on page 63.

- Some children will put non-food objects into their mouths. Care should be taken to ensure that any materials used are safe, in case children use them inappropriately.

If in any doubt about the appropriateness of physical contact in play, it is always better to err on the side of caution and not use it. Most of the activities in this book can be carried out without touching a child in any way.

Chapter 3
Supporting a shared understanding of other people

Children on the autism spectrum have difficulties in sharing thoughts, feelings, meanings, intentions and other mental experiences of living in the world. Although they find others intrinsically significant, they do not easily key in to normal social interactive behaviour. This results in the neglect of vital social and communicative information in normal everyday interactions, and sometimes in odd or even bizarre behaviour. Consequently, as the child grows and learns about the world, they may miss out on huge chunks of important information about how other people love, hate, fear and desire. They do not pick up on how others respond to similar experiences and then picture them in their minds.

Because they do not fully understand the shared nature of thinking and feeling, they may become somewhat detached from the social world. This detachment may take many forms, including aloofness, remoteness, a rigid intransigence, a distant or sometimes dreamy passivity, a fascination with unusual interests and an array of social behaviours that other people find strange. This lack of connectedness underlies the autistic condition.

Case study

Gareth hated windows being open and could not understand why other people not only tolerated this but voluntarily opened windows on hot days. What was important to Gareth seemed odd to the people around him.

For William, the sensory qualities of the plastic were the only thing that he wanted to talk about in the Design and Technology lesson. Whilst the other children were cutting, warming, bending, bonding and shaping it into animal forms, William simply wanted to stroke his cheek repeatedly with the plastic and to smell it. William failed to understand that the other children did not find the same satisfaction in the material. Although he clearly understood the design task, he found great difficulty in getting started and needed repeated reminders to progress with the task. In his mind, the salient qualities of the plastic were stronger than the desire for him to do the design task.

Both William and Gareth experienced thoughts and feelings related to their own experience, but lacked the feelings and thoughts that were equivalent to the other children around them.

A child unable to learn through a shared understanding will have an over-reliance on rational thinking, which leads to an unbalanced view of the world. By learning to share thoughts, feelings and experience, children on the autism spectrum can gain intellectual and emotional balance.

This chapter looks at how this imbalance can be addressed by helping the child to use their innate potential to learn with other people. In this way they will gain a better understanding of others and of a world that is socially organised.

This shared understanding relies on some key social skills:

- using eyes;
- sharing attention;
- feeling what other people feel and understanding emotions;
- making friends;
- proximity;
- taking turns and understanding groups;
- maintaining relationships;
- understanding what other people think;
- sharing interesting information;
- understanding facial expressions and body language.

Brief descriptions of these skills appear below, and these are followed by suggestions for strategies and activities to help develop the skills in different situations:

- playground and free-play time;
- one-to-one work;
- group-based sessions;
- in class.

Social skills for understanding others
Using eyes

Children with autism typically make less eye contact than normally developing children and may not use their eyes to attract attention, to direct other people's attention or to check that they have (or do not have) the attention of someone else. Some of these children over-use their eyes in communication: they will stare at the person they are talking to and do not know when to avert their gaze. Others will not look at the person they are talking to at all. Some may feel uneasy about the way an adult uses eye contact towards them. A more comfortable and normal use of gaze can be developed through the child's relationship with the teacher or other adult.

Children on the autism spectrum may need to be taught use of eyes, but it is important to avoid training them to make eye contact. If, for example, you gave them a reward only when they made eye contact, the action could become ritualised so that the child used gaze as a meaningless gesture when they wanted a reward. Instead, gaze should be used when the child implicitly understands that they are interacting with a person who has independent thoughts and intentions.

For children with autism to use natural eye contact and gaze, they need to have a strong reason to communicate, such as when they feel excited, angry, silly or frustrated. Spontaneous behaviour should therefore be encouraged. Where possible, find natural opportunities to develop this behaviour into a fluent and intuitive way of monitoring and directing attention.

Sharing attention

The ability to share attention with others and consequently to learn with them is a central difficulty experienced by children with autism. This might be manifested through averting the gaze, not attending to where someone else is looking or not following another person's train of thought — and consequently becoming confused by their language.

Similarly, to encourage the sharing of attention, the emphasis should be not on training and instruction, but on creating real reasons for attending to a shared focus. Make activities exciting; make the focus of group attention big and bright and the most interesting thing the children have seen that day.

Feeling what other people feel and understanding emotions

Children with autism often have difficulty in tuning into the feelings of others, and consequently in adapting their behaviour accordingly. There is some value in highlighting the facial expressions that are associated with various feelings, but without an empathetic understanding of emotions, the child with autism will find great difficulties in using this information. The strategies that follow promote an empathetic understanding of how other people feel; others build on this to help children think and reflect about why people do what they do.

Making friends

Many children with autism do have the same desire to share experience through friendship as normally developing children. Others, in particular those children with Asperger syndrome, often have the desire but lack the skills to make and maintain friendships. The following strategies are designed to structure the early development of this social orientation through the child sharing time and experience with others.

Proximity

Children with autism sometimes have difficulty in accepting people sitting or standing close to them. For others, the kind and reassuring touch that is often used to help children feel comfortable in their work and play can be deeply uncomfortable. These difficulties may be owing to particular sensory sensitivities, but many children are simply concerned about what the other person's intentions are. This can be resolved by careful and patient clarification. Some of the strategies that follow may help to reduce these sensitivities and clarify confusions about proximity.

Taking turns and understanding groups

Participating in groups can present problems for children on the autism spectrum. This is rarely because of difficulty in understanding the sequence involved in turn-taking activities; more usually it is because they find it hard to see the intentions of others as being real and equivalent. Consequently, they develop strategies to cope with taking turns, rather than working from an understanding of the social processes involved. The best way to help these children participate is therefore to help them acquire a better understanding of other people's perspective.

"TA – DAAAA"

Maintaining relationships

The issue of relationship breakdown is, of course, not exclusive to autism, but children on the autism spectrum have particular difficulties in this area. They lack many of the skills necessary to maintain relationships, and this often leads to misunderstandings and confusion. Young children and those with the greatest global learning difficulties can make huge demands of their parents, carers, teachers and therapists, and people often find it takes a long time to develop a meaningful relationship with them.

Food for thought

Interestingly, some parents see other people's children on the autism spectrum as being more emotionally detached than their own. This is because over time they have successfully established a meaningful and communicative relationship with their own child but still find other children distant and difficult to reach.

For older and more able children on the autism spectrum, relationship difficulties can be more subtle but just as pernicious. Conversational skills include listening, knowing what other people are interested in, taking turns in conversation, reading facial expressions and interpreting body language. Where these skills are lacking, the result is conversational breakdown or speech in monologue. The responsibility for the maintenance and repair of relationships clearly rests on those most able to cope with it, but this does not remove the responsibility of the child with autism to work towards effective and meaningful relationships.

Understanding what other people think

Children on the autism spectrum have difficulty in understanding that other people have thoughts that are independent of their own. More able children on the spectrum may show some ability to differentiate their thoughts from those of others, but even then they often lack an empathetic perspective. Recognising the thoughts of others is an advanced skill, but children on the autism spectrum generally lack the fundamental building blocks of the skill that would be found in a normally developing child. Even very able adults on the spectrum may lack the rudiments and have to rely on constructing a logical method of establishing people's thoughts and feelings, based on deduction and previous experience. The strategies overleaf are aimed at developing the beginnings of an empathetic understanding of what other people think.

'Effective relationships and a sense of connectedness can be developed and built on by sharing information that is of interest.'

Sharing interesting information

Effective relationships and a sense of connectedness can be developed and built on by sharing information that is of interest. When the child with autism approaches an adult or another child to share some information because they have a common interest in the subject, this is a landmark in the development of that child.

Case study

Lloyd enjoyed talking about wireless technology in computer networks and hacking strategies to access the security codes for major corporations. The teacher attempted to share this interest with Lloyd, although it stretched her understanding of computers to the limit. Through this, however, she was able to begin exploring how she and Lloyd both thought about things. They were able to compare each other's likes and dislikes about a range of subjects, and this eventually developed into discussions about bigger questions of morality and religion.

It is sometimes difficult to get a child to move beyond the stage of interacting with others to request something. Teaching plans should be designed to share information that is of importance to the child and to get them to share information with others. Interactions can be structured so that the child is more disposed to engage someone else in their thoughts and interests.

The strategies and activities below are designed to spur children on the autism spectrum into shared experience using their natural (but neglected) disposition towards interacting with other people.

Understanding facial expression and body language

Children with autism often find difficulty in understanding the thoughts, intentions and feelings of others through their use of body posture and facial expression. A similar difficulty in understanding the subtleties of this type of communication underlies the exaggerated or understated facial expressions sometimes seen in these children.

Strategies and activities for developing social skills

The following strategies and activities are grouped according to whether they develop skills normally acquired at an early or later stage of social development. In the early stage, children are encouraged to develop their understanding of other people and the basic skills of social communication. These skills include using and interpreting eye direction and facial expressions meaningfully, initiating communicative requests and comments, using imitation, and developing simple expectations of other people. In the later stage, the children are encouraged to develop a sophisticated understanding of other people and the skills associated with co-operating and collaborating, such as seeing others' point of view and making predictions about other people's actions in the past or future. In both stages, the teacher is aiming to use the child's inherent social capabilities so that their social skills become intuitive and automatic.

The early development strategies will be appropriate for some older and more able children who have not developed these skills at an intuitive level. It should be borne in mind that although some people with autism develop remarkable social skills – speaking articulately and interacting effectively with others in their social and business lives – sometimes these skills mask the difficulties they have in understanding subtle meanings and social timing. Most of the activities can be modified to suit the needs of children across the autism spectrum.

Playground or free-play time
Early development

- Play a peek-a-boo game by placing a cloth over your face. When the child looks towards you, remove the cloth with a joyful cheer or a surprised 'Boo!'
- While the child is playing, sit near them with an identical set of play materials and imitate the child's actions. If the child removes your play materials, start to play with their original materials.

- While the child is playing, introduce some complementary play and invite the child to play with you or adopt some of your ideas. For example, if the child is playing with a doll and pram, you might give the child a bottle and say, 'Baby . . . drink.'

- When the child requests something to play with, look in another direction until they manage to catch your eye. (This strategy can be used only when the child expects their other communicative attempts to be successful.)

- Play games that require a focus of attention. Activities that often work well with younger children include marbles running through pipes, water and sand play, blowing bubbles and playing with a jack-in-the-box. Older children are likely to have particular interests that should be incorporated into their games.

Case study

Marianne liked to record the football results every Saturday in her diary. She memorised many of the results each week and could answer questions about how many goals teams scored. The teacher introduced a fantasy football game in which Marianne chose her own players for a fantasy team. Marianne was able to discuss who had scored which goals and who had saved goals in the league games. This was used by the teacher to talk about how people work together in a team and how the personalities of players were similar to the personality dynamics of her class. This became the focus that Marianne and the teacher shared for a few weeks and one that Marianne remembered for much longer.

- Use interactive play – such as tickle games, rough-and-tumble play and chasing games. Introduce exaggerated facial expressions and dramatic tension to make them exciting and engaging. Repeat these often, developing new variations on previous games to maintain interest.

Later development

- Allow plenty of opportunity for children with autism to play with toys and do activities that other children also find attractive. The task is for the children to negotiate the use of these toys and activities, based on a shared understanding. This encourages them to focus on what the other child is thinking or feeling – which might be, for example, 'I want what you have', 'I'm looking at it', 'I'll wait until you look elsewhere' or 'If you do it again I will be angry.' Sometimes this interaction will be tolerant and co-operative, with each child taking notice of how others differ in their use of objects; sometimes it will be noisy and confrontational. Remember that confrontation is as useful for a child learning about the thoughts, feelings and desires of others as are tolerance and co-operation. Just how confrontational it is allowed to become will be a matter for your own judgement.

'Remember that confrontation is as useful for a child learning about the thoughts and feelings of others as are tolerance and co-operation.'

- Provide activities that require two or more children to work together to complete a task. For example, do a jigsaw, giving each child some pieces which they have to put in; play with a marble run, taking turns to place balls at the top; throw and catch or roll a ball to each other; or throw a paper aeroplane to each other.

One-to-one work
Early development

- Sitting in the room and gradually moving nearer to the child is a necessary first step for some children with autism.

- Always make your intention clear to the child as you approach them.

- Offer the child something moderately attractive but not highly salient. (Where the salience is too great, the child will focus only on the object and not on the process of interaction.) Watch the child at a comfortable distance. Do not attempt to remove objects from the child during this period.

- Some children do not like being touched; some like to touch you only when they want to and not necessarily when you want them to; some will tolerate touch and proximity if they understand why you have approached them. Some children enjoy touch, but it has to be a firm hold rather than a gentle pat or stroke.

- Build up the child's expectation by blowing soap bubbles and allowing the child to watch them fall to the floor. When this pattern is established, break the routine by pausing before blowing a bubble. The child should check why nothing is happening by looking at your eyes to see where you are looking. The bubbles must then be blown immediately. Re-establish the original pattern before repeating the pause.

- Many nursery rhymes, action songs and simple games are suitable for building up the child's expectations of a tickle or other action that they enjoy. When a rhyme or game is introduced, it should be used until the child shows signs of anticipation and pleasure. At this point, increase the delay before the final action and use exaggerated facial expressions, posture and voice to increase the affective anticipation of the child. The child may then make spontaneous eye contact, and this is used to trigger the final action.

- Use rough-and-tumble and tickle games to allow the children to become accustomed to touch. Use firm, not gentle, touch.

- Use a puppet (something like a monster or dinosaur) or put on a mask, and chase the child when they request this by giving you a mutually understood sign.

- At random times throughout the day, show pictures, models, photos or objects that the child finds very attractive. As they appear, get the child's attention with a pointed finger and explicit looking, and say, 'Look . . . a helicopter/lorry/shark/train.' Eventually the child may automatically associate the looking and the exclamation with getting the attention of others. If this is slow to develop, it may be accelerated by a different adult prompting the child's hand into a pointing gesture when the stimulus appears. It may be necessary to prompt some children to touch the teacher's hand to get their attention before using the pointing gesture.

- When you want the child to see your expression, draw their attention to it either by saying explicitly, for example, 'Look, I'm smiling – I am happy!' or by catching the child's eye and allowing them to take an interest in the different facial expressions that are used in emotional situations.

○ Use exaggerated facial expression and body language in drama and play. Look angry, sad, happy, excited or scared to draw the child's attention.

Later development

○ List all the things that the child does well. Then add all the positive things that they have tried hard to do. List all the things they have done that are helpful to others. List all the things that you both enjoy doing. Now list some of the occasions when you have enjoyed spending time together. Look together at photos of the things on your list, and spend some time revisiting some. Does the child understand that they think differently from other individuals? Do they assume (implicitly) that all people have thoughts that are independent of their own? Encourage them to understand that others may or may not have the same thoughts as they do.

○ Blindfold the child and then give them verbal instructions to guide them around the room to pick up an object. Then change roles so that you or another adult is blindfolded.

○ The child sits opposite the adult. The adult looks at a picture and the child guesses what it might show, based on the adult's descriptions.

○ Offer the child choices. If the child has problems making choices, start with a choice between two options, one of which is attractive and the other not. Later transfer this requesting to photocards, so that the child gives you the card with a photo of what they want. As the child becomes able to cope with simple choices, increase the range of options available and start to include some less concrete choices, such as 'Do you want to be Goldilocks or Daddy Bear?' When the child is confident that they can reliably make requests using a photocard, you can pretend not to understand and make lots of mistakes, giving similar objects of different size, colour or function. The child must repeatedly redefine their request.

○ Watch the child's favourite video or DVD; pause and ask what will happen next. Screenshots of two alternatives can be shown to assist the choice.

○ Play Twenty Questions: ask the child to guess what you are thinking about by asking up to 20 questions. You can only answer 'yes', 'no' or 'sometimes'.

○ Use action rhymes and songs with animals, people or imaginary creatures who show their feelings explicitly in the way they walk and speak; for example, 'A giant goes like this . . .' or 'I went to school one morning and I jumped like this.'

○ Go on an imaginary journey by drawing a map. Along the route, draw pictures of events that make the child happy, sad and so on, and ask them to show you how this looks, for example by making a happy face. If there are parts of the story that the child can enact, ask them to demonstrate.

Group-based sessions
Early development

○ Social behaviour in which the child positively engages with others should be gently but persistently encouraged with fun, laughter, cajoling and coaxing. This might include a huge range of behaviours such as sitting down with other children, asking a question, making a request, collaborating on a worksheet or waiting quietly for a few moments while someone else is speaking. Children on the autism spectrum do best in a supportive and structured environment in which everybody tries to remain cheerful and buoyant.

○ During snack-time, pause before handing the child the snack they have requested and wait for eye contact. Do not hold the snack within easy view of the child or their attention may be directed towards the food rather than to you.

○ Some children get too close and infringe personal space. Simple rules such as 'stand at one arm's distance from someone you are trying to talk to' can be helpful. Issues such as this can be included in discussion during PSHE lessons.

Later development

○ Share experiences emotionally. Celebrate the child's achievements and show delight in their interests. Also, on occasions, carefully show distress when something goes wrong.

○ In activities where children do something in turns, work in strict order from left to right, ensuring that children all wait their turn. Stop occasionally and ask the child to say who has the next turn. When there is an opportunity, change the order so that turns are taken from right to left.

○ For older and more able children, role play can be used to highlight and practise the subtleties of eye contact, including gaze aversion, timing, directing attention towards others and maintaining attention. The child is asked to think about a particular aspect of eye contact and to practise this in a supportive environment. This strategy does not seek to change the intuitive use of gaze, but to give the skills to interpret and communicate more effectively. For example, a child acting in role as a frustrated customer could be thinking about using eye contact to direct the shop assistant. The role play could be video recorded, and the best examples of eye contact could be shown to the class and used as a point of discussion.

○ Bring a large bag into the group. Indicate that everyone should be quiet, creating, if possible, silent tension to raise anticipation. Carefully take out a mystery object from the bag and, just before it emerges, show exaggerated expressions and make sounds to convey your feelings about the object. If the object is something that everyone likes, give a huge smile and laugh or clap. Otherwise you may show revulsion, horror or wickedness. The children should see that this object makes you feel excited or joyful or fearful or disgusted. As the children see the object for the first time, animate it and respond accordingly, so that they feel the affective resonance. If it is a spider or a snake, wriggle it towards them, saying 'Look out!' If it is a toy aeroplane, 'fly' it around their heads, showing pleasure as it dives past the children's attempts to catch it.

○ Hide an object that the child wants in one of three boxes. Show the three boxes to the class whilst staring at the one containing the object. Then move the three boxes to different places around the room. Everyone stares at the box that hides the object. Ask the child if they can find the item. As a variation on this activity, the object is hidden in the hands of someone in the group, and everyone looks at that person. See if the child can find the hidden object by using the visual cue.

- Pretend to be asleep and let the children be monsters that wake you up in the night.
- Give some pretend food to the child, who then hands it out to other children – pretending to be the zoo keeper feeding animals in the zoo.
- Practise naming other children by looking at photos, then naming real children in the group.
- One child is asked to hide outside the classroom. Ask, 'Who is missing?' If the children find this difficult, have a look at a photo of all the children in the class and then ask, 'Is she here? Where is she? Is he here? Where is he?' The activity can be repeated for a child who is absent from school that day.
- In a group, ask each child to bring an object, photo or piece of news from home. Then ask questions to see if they remember what everyone said; for example, 'What did Alison say?', 'Did Lee go to the seaside or did he play with his pet rabbit?' Alternatively, everybody names their favourite colour, animal or toy, then you ask the group, 'Can you remember what [child's name] said?'
- Ask an adult to leave the room. While they are gone, ask the child to hide something, such as a bag, that belongs to the adult. When the adult returns, they ask if anyone can help them find the object.
- The game of I Spy can be used to help the child understand that what is in their head may not be the same as the thoughts of others.

In class
Early development
- Look for opportunities to make eye contact with the child throughout the day.
- Sit with the child while they are working. Show an interest in what they are doing or looking at. Name the things that they are involved with, using single words or short phrases.
- Celebrate successes in the child's work with a brief smile and then look away. This helps the child to understand that adult attention is not always intended to prevent them from doing as they wish.
- Watch video, theatre or pantomime together, sharing the fun, fear and dramatic tension.

Later development
- Use the child's name to get their attention before speaking to them; for example, 'Imran . . . can you tell me . . .'
- Ask the child to hand out items such as writing books, pens and drinking cups to other children.
- Have the child sit in a semi-circle and take their turn to come out and demonstrate an activity or try something.
- Introduce new items of information, using an association with a favourite object, word or image. For example, a favourite helicopter toy could be used to deliver letters in the Literacy lesson; or, if the child likes the sound of a

"Give the drama lots of life and energy!"

particular word such as 'sizzling', you could find a way of introducing it into the lesson or dialogue to draw the child's attention.

○ Enact stories or familiar scenes from fairy tales, historical adventures, religious stories from around the world or a favourite video. Improvise costumes and make simple props. Show exaggerated expressions and give the drama lots of life and energy.

○ If everyone is comfortable with animals, bring a friendly dog or other pet into the group. Allow the awareness of each other's emotions to spread and increase through the group, and encourage the child to engage with these shared feelings. Care and vigilance must, of course, be observed to maintain the optimal affective levels amongst the children and to protect the children and the animal from danger. It is important that you feel confident about managing the children and the animal in this situation.

○ In a short drama based around a familiar story, ask the child to take on different roles; for example, 'Yesterday you were the angry giant, but today you are Jack, and you will be frightened when you hear the giant roar.' Or, in a drama based on a Victorian school, you could ask the child to play a Victorian school child, then the strict teacher and then a parent who has just emerged from a shift in the mill. It may be possible to encourage some children to reflect on their experiences within the different roles. A child who has difficulty in using this vocabulary may be helped by being offered a simple choice; for example, 'Did you [or the name of the character] feel angry or frightened?' If you can record the drama on video, this may be used to help the child reflect on their role.

○ The children should be given a task that will fuel their own ambitions, using materials that are highly attractive. In this case the children must work together to build something bigger and better than either of them could achieve independently. The shared learning must focus on collaboration, negotiation and pleasure in the contribution that each child makes. For more able children, the focus of engagement may be around a shared interest in collecting objects, or numbers, or a shared sense of humour, or talking about specific items. Allowing these interests to develop requires allocation of time and resources.

○ Sometimes, for no apparent reason, a child who is fully engaged in an activity will stop and disengage for a few moments. If this happens, prompt the child to encourage them to re-engage.

○ At the end of a lesson, talk about or show something associated with the most interesting thing that happened in it. Reviewing the lesson in this way allows the children to reflect upon it and perhaps comment on their learning.

Chapter 4
Supporting communication

Some children with autism spectrum conditions have communication difficulties that are very severe and involve a lack of functional speech and non-verbal communicative expressions. In other children, the difficulties are less severe, involving the inability to understand the subtleties of language and the thoughts and feelings of others. They may develop speech, but this may be unusually limited in its use, particularly in informal circumstances, or it may have an atypical quality.

For all children on the autism spectrum, it is important to develop the desire to communicate as well as the skills and understanding of the process that will enable them to make progress.

Food for thought
Whilst shopping with one child as part of a social skills programme, his persistent and noisy insistence that we should buy every bottle of washing-up liquid on the shelf made me re-think the idea that the drive to communicate is weak in children with autism.

Normally developing children use language to exchange thoughts, feelings and intentions about objects and events, and generally enjoy exploring how other people respond to shared ideas and feelings about things. Children on the autism spectrum either do not generally engage in this exchange of information, or engage in ways that are guided by their different interests in the world and its sensory and social qualities. Some children do develop a sense of social connection, but still have difficulty in starting a conversation, keeping it going, or knowing when to stop and allow the other person to speak.

For children who find communication very difficult, the communicative environment needs to be adapted. The people most closely associated with the child agree to interpret particular behaviour as intentional communication and respond accordingly. As the skills of the child increase, the responsibility for making the communication successful gradually transfers back to the child. Eventually child and adult should share the responsibility equally. The aim is for the child to develop an implicit desire to share information with others because it feels good. From this position, the child can build their communication skills on a social basis.

'It is important to accept whatever communicative attempts the child makes.'

It is important to accept whatever communicative attempts the child makes, so it may be worth giving them opportunities to learn about a number of communicative systems. Some of these will have advantages over others in some settings, but disadvantages in others.

Using visual communication
Children who have difficulty in communicating in ways that are typical for normally developing children may benefit from using visual methods of communication. These can be used to communicate in a wide variety of situations; for example, about work that needs completing, about items that

are available to request, about the events of the day, and what will happen in the lesson. Reference can be made back to visual methods if the child loses attention or doesn't listen well. Objects, symbols, photos or the written word may be used. Many children on the autism spectrum are trained how to use this type of communication or have learnt to do it themselves because it is a useful way of maintaining someone else's attention. Others learn it through imitation. Visual communication can take several forms, as described below.

Objects

Objects are often helpful for younger or less-communicative children. They provide a meaningful and physical reminder that doesn't disappear as speech does.

Case study

For Beth, handing someone an empty cup had more meaning than a spoken word or a photo when she wanted a drink. For this reason a plastic cup was left out for Beth so that she could make a request. After this behaviour was established, the cup was sawn down its length so that it looked less like a real cup. The open side was then glued to a card, which showed a symbol of a cup and a bottle. The cup was then removed and the card was exchanged for a drink.

Symbols and photographs

Both symbols and photos are useful for communication, and each have advantages and disadvantages.

Symbols are more easily generalised between one object or concept and another. For some children, a photo represents exactly that object and may not represent another similar object of the same type but of slightly different appearance. A symbol, on the other hand, is more easily taken to mean 'any item of this type'. Symbols are particularly useful for communicating about invisible items or abstract ideas; for example, you could have a symbol for the wind, tasty, poorly, beautiful, or 'No, thank you'. Symbols are also useful for communicating about going to places and doing things for the first time – when a photo may not be available. Symbols, however, lack the immediacy of photos, which are quickly understood by many children, need less teaching time and usually facilitate communication with greater fluency.

Photos have become very popular since digital photography and low-cost laminators have made them easy and relatively inexpensive to produce. A photo can be taken, edited, printed, laminated and fixed on the wall – within minutes. A symbol could be ambiguous and potentially confusing, but a photo is usually more easily understood. Even for children who have sufficient language to communicate most of their needs, photos can be used to communicate when they are confused or anxious.

If an object is no longer appropriate or available, the corresponding card can be removed. Cards can also be useful for encouraging children to take turns in requesting, as the adult can only respond to one request at a time.

Using request cards

Here are some ideas for introducing and making use of request cards:

○ Find something worth communicating about. This might be a favourite snack food, a toy or perhaps time on the computer. Take a photo of the child using the object or participating in the event. If more than one child might use the photo, then show just the object. The photo (or, alternatively, symbol) can be used as a request card.

○ Photocards could be introduced to a child in a group in which some children understand simple language. Allow them to watch as you ask the other children to give the request card to you. As soon as the card is given, hand over whatever is being requested. If the child does not quickly pick up how to use this method, an additional adult can be used to guide their hand to the card and then give it to you.

○ As the child begins to understand that they can request familiar objects in context, you can generalise the request cards to other settings; for example, from school to home or from one adult to another. Introduce additional cards so that the child can build up a vocabulary of things that they are confident about requesting.

○ Once the child has an expectation that their requests will be met, the request cards can be stored somewhere easily accessible for them. The cards could be kept together in a box or folder, but many children prefer to have them more visible. They could be displayed in horizontal or vertical strips in a place frequently visited by the child. Velcro® is good for attaching the cards.

○ Once the child is familiar with using the cards in this way, they should be encouraged to make frequent requests throughout the day. Children with autism need to have as many opportunities for communicating as normally developing children do. Create opportunities for communication so that, for example, the child has to request food items for lunch or parts of a toy to reconstruct. The cards can also be used to break a sequence down. Going for a walk to the park or to the playground may be broken down into: coat, outside shoes, park, swings. This creates at least four opportunities to practise the transfer of communicative information and so helps to build expectations of successful communication.

○ Photographic keyfobs or compact photograph albums could be used as a portable communication aid.

○ For children who can read written words, word cards can replace photos or symbols. They can be made into lists or diary items and ticked off as the work is completed.

Many children on the autism spectrum make speedy progress with the cards and become accomplished at requesting. As they become more able to understand the implicit expectations of others and gain experience of the sharing of information and the joy of successful engagement with others, they become more likely to communicate their interest in something without expecting to get it.

'Find something worth communicating about.'

Jerome had already been asked not to use the word 'telephone' to tease one of the other children in the class. He took great pleasure in finding devious ways of introducing the word into a conversation. Upon finding that he gained repeated attention each time he pointed and preceded a statement with 'Look, it's a . . . ', Jerome quickly learned to produce many variations on the theme of 'Look, that is not a telephone' and 'Look, that has a bell . . . like a telephone.' Later, when the novelty of the word 'telephone' had worn off, Jerome found he could communicate on a whole range of subjects.

If the child has a particular fascination with something, you can use it to accelerate this process with the following strategies:

○ If the child is fascinated by, for example, aeroplanes, show them an aeroplane card when you hear one passing over. Take them to the window to see it, repeatedly pointing to the sky and to the card. Show the child your great excitement and enthusiasm for the aeroplane and let your enthusiasm transfer to the child. When the child has built up an expectation of this excitement, allow the child to go to the card first and show it to you before you become excited about the aeroplane.

○ Collect pictures, books, photos and models associated with the child's interest. At some point during the day, perhaps in a Literacy hour or a quiet reading time, introduce a 'sharing interest' time. Hide one of the objects – for example, if the child's interest were tractors, you might hide a toy tractor – then show the child a photo of the object. Point to the photo with enthusiasm, saying, 'Look, a tractor!' Start a search for the item, saying, for example, 'Look, over here . . . is it in the box? No. Look over there. I can see it sticking out from behind the bookcase!' When the object is retrieved, continue to show interest and talk about it, pointing out details and perhaps asking questions.

The aim of using request cards is to build up the skills needed in communication, and the strategies should be used alongside other means of communication. The choice of these should be decided in consultation with those most closely associated with the child. Communication will work most effectively if all those around the child can understand the methods being used. It may be helpful to consult a professional skilled in communication development in children on the autism spectrum, such as a speech and language therapist, speech pathologist, specialist teacher or psychologist.

Other strategies that have been successful with some children include:
○ sign language – usually Makaton;
○ electronic communicators that use recorded or computer-synthesised voices when the child presses a button or types in a word.

Things worth communicating about

An important aspect of developing communication is to key in to the things that the child finds engaging or stimulating – and what is salient to children with

'An important aspect of developing communication is to key in to the things that the child finds engaging or stimulating.'

autism spectrum conditions may appear unusual or bizarre to others. Some children, for example, find revolving objects fascinating and will concentrate for remarkable lengths of time on the spinning motion. Other children on the autism spectrum find the sounds of particular words funny, exhilarating or sometimes frightening. Others become deeply absorbed in detailed information on a subject not usually of interest to children of their age, such as the life history of Baroness Thatcher. Young children and those with more severe autism are often interested in perceptual processes such as tickling, spinning, bouncing and rocking. These movements can be incorporated into the programme for each child so that they can be requested and communicated about. Sequences of such movements can be incorporated into physical play (see Chapter 5) or used within taught subjects such as science or mathematics.

Many children on the autism spectrum have an interest in building and construction materials. These are easy to use as a means of requesting and, later, discussing and negotiating. More linguistically able children may benefit from having their interests incorporated into their studies. A child with an interest in capital cities of the world may find a greater willingness to communicate in school if the curriculum is modified to refer to these places.

Developing skills

Once the child has developed simple communication, the next stage is to help them to think flexibly using words, to communicate these thoughts and feelings, and to reflect on the experience of others. Here are further strategies and activities that may help in developing language and communication skills in children on the autism spectrum. They are not in strict order of developmental difficulty and, like most of the suggestions in this book, they are intended to stimulate a creative approach to working with children on the autism spectrum rather than teaching a programme of skills.

Strategies for early communication

- Engage with the child by imitating their vocalisations and movements. The aim is for the child to respond to your imitation by increasing the variety and frequency of intentional behaviour.

- Interpret the child's reaching towards an object as intentional pointing by retrieving the object and giving it to the child.

- Respond sensitively to the child's actions. For example, if the child picks up a cup, treat this as an intentional request for a drink; if the child stands near to their coat, interpret this as a request to go out. This may seem an obvious strategy, but the point is that the child needs to be observed closely and constantly, so that important – and sometimes infrequent – opportunities to learn about communication are not lost. In a busy classroom, it is very easy to miss the occasional opportunities.

- Wait for the child to make eye contact before giving a requested object. This will usually work if their expectation to hand it over has not been met.

- Sing a song and miss out the endings of some of the lines.

Strategies for communication development for verbal children

○ Find an object that is interesting for the child, and point to and name all the parts as you follow where the child is looking.

○ Make a trail of partially hidden objects that are interesting for the child. As you walk round together, point and say, 'Look, it's a . . . ' Use your enthusiasm for the discovery to encourage the child to imitate.

○ As the child requests an object, give them opportunities to extend their communication; for example, 'Yes, which one? Red or blue?' or 'Yes, ask Jenny.'

○ Write a real-life story for the child about something that happened to them using handwriting or cartoon-style pictures. Talk about the story, asking questions such as, 'What happened when he did that to you?', 'What happened next?', 'OK, let's draw that . . . ', 'Which one did you prefer?'

○ Make a fantasy map showing the journey of a fictitious character – for example, taking a route through a system of underground caves, or going on an undersea exploration, or walking through a dark forest on a dark night with an unreliable torch. Talk about the journey and the adventures the character has on the way, asking questions such as, 'Can you tell me what it would look like?', 'What could [the character] hear?', 'How would he escape from there?'

○ Use construction materials to make a special machine or new invention. Ask, 'What could it be?', 'What would you use this part for?', 'How could you make it flyproof/waterproof/fire-resistant/stronger?'

○ Hold a picture so the child cannot see it. Ask if they can guess what you are looking at by listening to your clues. For example, for a picture of an egg, you might say, 'Hmm. I like to eat this at breakfast time. It comes in a shell. It is laid by a hen.' For some children, you will have to give a specific instruction, such as, 'Tell me what I am looking at' or '[Child's name], I am talking about an . . . '

○ Video the child talking about their favourite subject in front of a small group. Watch the video with the child and praise all their positive communications, so that the child can see themselves as others see them. You might use phrases such as, 'Good, you paused there to allow everyone to look at the object', 'Well done, you looked at her eyes and listened without speaking when she asked you a question.'

○ If the child insists on talking about the same subject every time they have a conversation, use this as a basis for broadening the conversation. If the child is interested in tractors, for example, talk about farmers who drive tractors, tractor-like wheels that are on other vehicles, or farm animals that see the tractor working.

○ If the child repeatedly asks the same question and is reluctant to stray from this strategy, attempt to identify the trigger for this behaviour. It may be caused by underlying anxiety or confusion, or it may be that the child needs greater stimulation because they do not emotionally or intellectually engage with the activity.

'Use reading as a means of encouraging the child to use their speaking voice.'

○ As the child is starting to switch fluently between sorting objects into different groups by different features (things with wheels or things with wings, red things or blue things, 2D or 3D things), increase the expectation that they should communicate using two or three words together, such as 'blue aeroplane' or 'red bird flying'.

○ Use reading as a means of encouraging the child to use their speaking voice.

○ Design an activity that excites the child but can only be completed if the child asks someone else for something. For example, if the child enjoys playing with a toy train track, give half of the track to them and half to someone else. Encourage them to talk to each other and negotiate the organisation.

○ Play a game where the child is encouraged to imitate the adult's actions – such as touching heads or tapping knees. Then introduce a vocal action such as 'Boo!' into the sequence.

○ Hide an object in the room when the child is outside. When they return, ask them if they know where the object is hidden. Ask the other children where the child thinks it is. Ask the child to think of somewhere that the object could be hidden and to look in that place for the object. Ask the other children where the child thought it was. Did they find it there?

○ Put two children on either side of a screen or large piece of furniture and give one child a picture. As that child describes the picture, the other child must attempt to draw it on paper. When it is finished, they can compare the original with the newly drawn picture. It can be explained to them that the differences are there because they each have slightly different pictures in their minds – which can be made more similar by better communication. This could lead into a discussion about improving speaking and listening skills.

Chapter 5
Supporting play and creativity

Children with autism spectrum conditions have often been seen as having a poor imagination, little interest in play and a lack of spontaneity and creativity. In recent years, however, there has been an increased understanding of this and of what can be done to develop it. Indeed, creativity can be seen in many severely autistic and rigid thinkers.

Nevertheless, using the creative part of the mind to understand a social and communicative world is not usually a strength in people on the autism spectrum, and herein lies one key to helping children learn more effectively. Children with autism need to be helped to develop their creative abilities so that they can think more flexibly about increasingly complex and abstract ideas – including how they relate to the world, how others relate to it and how we all relate to each other. Through play and creativity, children with autism gain opportunities to view the world from different perspectives and to develop their understanding of the complexities of the social and intentional world. The play-drama strategies and activities in this chapter are designed to structure the learning of children with autism spectrum conditions towards this goal.

Engaging with others because it is fun!

At the heart of this approach to the education of children with autism is the idea that we engage with others because it is exciting to do so. To interact because of desire for food or toys or a favourite video is important, but this does not tackle the central difficulty in autism. Play and creativity with children on the autism spectrum begins with encouraging the experience of fun and excitement with others. Building on this foundation are three stages of development:

1 **Establishing representations** – focusing on a shared engagement in exciting and meaningful actions, language and objects.
2 **Integrating ideas** – incorporating these actions and objects into more complex sequences or narratives.
3 **Developing sub-plots within the narrative** – using ideas as the focus of shared interest and manipulating them into less concrete and intangible forms such as fantasy.

Activities, teaching structures and strategies to support development at each stage are suggested below.

It is important not to make assumptions about the abilities and capabilities of those with autism spectrum conditions. For older children it may be appropriate to use very early teaching structures; for some children it may be appropriate to use several structures at any one time.

The child's understanding of language is one indicator of where to start in teaching play and creativity. For children who have an understanding of speech at a very simple single-word level or below, the first group of activities may be the most appropriate place to start. Children with autism who can understand requests such as 'Give the blue ball to Kirsty', or who are able to understand simple stories or follow a simple dialogue, should be capable of working on the activities in the second group. Children who can understand the majority of language used towards them in sentence form may be suited to the activities in the third group.

Remember, however, that children with autism may mislead others through displaying language skills at a higher level than their actual understanding of the words and their social implications. It may be necessary to discuss their level of development with a speech and language therapist, specialist teacher or psychologist experienced in assessing children with autism and autism spectrum conditions.

You may find it difficult to be convincing in play. Many adults find it makes them feel very vulnerable, particularly if the child with autism does not respond positively or immediately. It can be helpful to work only with trusted adults who have a good sense of humour – at least until any initial reluctance to protect oneself from ridicule has been overcome, and replaced with the sense of sharing a moment of fun and excitement with the child or children.

Activities to support play and creativity
1 Early play and creativity: establishing representations
With all these games, you are searching for ways to:

- engage the child within a shared narrative;
- encourage requests from the child for repeats;
- establish shared expectations and then sabotage them – this often triggers social communication behaviour such as eye contact and expressions of surprise that can be developed and refined.

Here I come!
Find a sensory activity that the child enjoys. This might involve tickling their arms and shoulders, bouncing with them while holding hands, running quickly or using their favourite words or sounds. Develop a short narrative sequence that uses this sensory activity and build it up to a high point; for example, you could:

- count, 1, 2, 3 . . . then chase;
- hide under a sheet and then emerge towards the child;
- say, 'Ready, steady, go . . .' (coming down the slide or jumping off the step);
- wave a particular object such as a damp cloth, a large glove or a favourite puppet at them . . . and then engage with their response.

The preliminary actions are used to signal to the child that a special play event is about to happen. Once these are introduced, they need to be repeated until

"Work with trusted adults with a good sense of humour . . ."

they become part of the routines established between you and the child. Through this the child builds an expectation of the event narrative, which you can use to develop new ways of engaging.

Sometimes the child may engage with the activity but not with the social features, such as anticipatory tension; pleasure from facial expressions; or using eye contact, exaggerated play actions, spoken language or smiling. If the sensory activity has itself become too salient, it may obscure the social opportunities and prevent the child from engaging socially. In this case the activity may need to be modified or even abandoned.

'If the sensory activity has itself become too salient, it may obscure the social opportunities.'

Explore

Choose some objects that are interesting to the child, and hide them in a sand tray so that the child finds them and then starts to search intentionally for them. For example, if the child is interested in vehicles, hide lots of different types of toy vehicles – ones that they particularly like and some that they are unfamiliar with. Do not hide vehicles that are so salient that they prevent the child from exploring further. Alternatively, hide these items so that they will not be found as quickly as others.

As a next stage, introduce additional items that might suggest that some of the objects should be played with together. If the child is interested in vehicles, you could hide toy people to sit in a car, a railway track for a train, a digger for excavating the sand, a box with a hinged lid to act as a garage or animals to go in a horsebox. Sometimes it is useful to hide unconnected items that might trigger an unexpected response. Hiding a toy animal such as a spider might work with some children.

As an alternative activity, set up a parallel sand tray with identical objects and imitate the child's actions with the objects to establish a sense of connectedness. Then introduce some events within your sand tray that catch the child's attention. For example, you might discover a new object and show how excited you are about it. Or you might show that the vehicles can be re-hidden by covering them with dry sand, then play an exaggerated hide-and-seek game, hiding and rediscovering the vehicles.

In this way, you are joining in with the child's play by introducing new and interesting objects into their narrative. As these are taken over by the child, you can introduce additional items. When the child wants to take over a new object, use it as an opportunity to develop social communication skills. (See Chapters 3 and 4 for strategies.)

Search

Hide one of the child's favourite objects. Make a symbol card or take a photo of the hiding place. The child searches in the place indicated on the card. Re-hide the object in another place if the child is willing to relinquish it, or wait a short while and invite them to search for another, more interesting object.

The next stage is to hide a series of cards around the room that ultimately lead to the correct hiding place. Begin to use words to label the hiding place. These might start with very simple instructions, such as, 'in the yellow cupboard', 'under Teddy' or 'in the sink'. Later, this might be extended to more sophisticated phrases, such as 'near the big window' or 'inside Jacob's bag'.

Black bag

Hide a number of moderately interesting objects inside a large bag. Sit the child near the bag and start to pull out an object, preceding the action with exaggerated facial and vocal expressions. For example, a plastic tiger might be preceded by expressions of fear, a teddy bear by affectionate sighs and loving smiles, a rubber lizard by squeals – to be followed by excited laughter as it tickles your hand and climbs up your arm.

Face masks

Approach the child, wearing a rubber face mask. Allow the child to remove it if they wish to and can do so safely. Some children may be anxious about this; if this is likely, use the activity with suitable caution. Allowing them to play with the face mask first will allow them to see what it is and become familiar with it. Other children may be better starting with a smaller modification to your appearance, such as a hat, headscarf, eye-patch, false moustache or plastic red nose. These can allow the child time to get used to the idea that appearances can be temporarily changed.

When the child is comfortable with you wearing a face mask, use some other masks showing different characters and moods – such as happy, kind and gentle, or scary. Change the way you walk and talk according to the character suggested by the mask. Many children with autism spectrum conditions have been negatively affected because they have been surprised by someone dressing up – as a clown or Santa, for example – so great sensitivity should be used with this activity.

Rough-and-tumble bears

Throw a cloak of fake fur over yourself and crouch on the ground, pretending to be a bear. When the children come near, growl quietly and try to reach a child with one paw. Don't try very hard at first, but as the children become used to 'the bear', try harder to grab them. Approach the children and growl more loudly. Any children caught by the bear are rolled onto the floor and the bear pretends to eat them. (See Chapter 2 for guidance on child protection issues in physical games.)

Twirly python

Twist a large cotton sheet into a 'python'. Make it snake towards the child, then wind it around the child's body. Continue this action so that the child starts to spin slowly round. Stop and unwind the child before they become dizzy. Suitable precautions should be taken to safeguard the child, including steadying them and working on a soft, flat floor surface.

Whirly winds and sudden snow

Waft a white cotton sheet, singing, 'Here comes the wind, here comes the wind, here comes the wind and here comes the snow.' On the word 'snow', drop the sheet onto the child's head and body. Then shake the sheet around the child, accompanied by wintry gale noises. Remove the sheet and prepare to repeat the game.

Singing songs

The use of music and singing is a highly effective way of establishing both a narrative and a sense of connectedness with the child, as you and the child have a shared focus on the songs. For some non-verbal children, this will simply mean that you sing their favourite songs.

Sing a familiar song and pause before the end of the line. Encourage the child to sing the words required to finish the song. Alternatively, establish the narrative by singing the correct words, then try out alternative words to see if the child responds to the modification. For example, you might sing, 'If I were a butterfly' and then substitute 'aeroplane' for 'butterfly'. Take the child's response and use this to develop social communication skills and a revised narrative by incorporating it into the song. For example, if the child says, 'Not aeroplane . . . butterfly!', you can say, 'Oops, I'm sorry, you are right – it is butterfly', then repeat the verse making other mistakes. Alternatively, the child might say, 'spaceship', and then you could use this idea by allowing the children to make spaceship noises or actions.

Objects

Watch the child playing with objects, remember some of the ideas that they take most interest in, then construct a narrative based on these interests:

- If the child likes vehicles and animals, combine these so that the animals join the vehicle on its journey, one at a time. They could ride on the vehicle or growl at it as it passes.
- If the child likes crashing, take two toy cars and race them around, trying to crash them against each other or into other objects.
- If the child is interested in revolving objects, such as wheels, encourage them to extend their play by introducing new, attractive items that can be used to develop it further. These might include toys that have increasingly large wheels or large numbers of wheels, or toys with rotor blades or propellers.
- If the child is interested in chase games, extend this using puppets. You and the child each have a puppet, then chase each other trying to snarl, stalk, trap and catch the other's puppet.

In these activities, the child is being focused on the social interaction around objects. Remember that objects have a tendency to be overly salient and are sometimes used to the exclusion of people, so try to ensure that the object does not obscure the social opportunities.

2 Integrating ideas

In these activities, the child is given an opportunity to engage in a shared narrative that combines objects, language and sensory and rhythmic events. The child develops their understanding of others by working through play events that combine symbolic pretence, language and narratives.

Spider in the box

This activity is useful for gaining the child's attention and developing social communication skills. Start with something that the child understands, for example you might take a biscuit tin that the child associates with snack-time and replace the biscuits with a large, rubber spider. As you open the lid, show great surprise or even shock – and then pretend to prevent the spider from escaping. Unfortunately, this particularly agile spider manages to climb quickly up your arm and on to your shoulders. You attempt to stop the spider but, alas, it escapes and runs over the child, tickling as it goes.

If the children are comfortable with this level of pretence and surprise, you can proceed to a symbolic level. To do this, the spider in the box narrative is repeated, but with an imaginary spider. You make the same expressions of surprise and attempts to contain the spider, even though it cannot be seen. The children should be carried by the familiar narrative, convinced by your expressions of emotion, and start to act in accordance with the imaginary scenario.

If the children are able to follow a non-existent creature through a familiar narrative, the characteristics of the imaginary spider can be changed and the children encouraged to see it in different ways. For example, you might uncover the spider to find that it is . . . enormous, beautiful, speedy, ferocious, flying, poorly, hungry or frightened. This has to be led convincingly, using lots of expression to make the spider's attributes and your responses clear. Finally, you can give a child the biscuit box and ask what they can find inside it. Ask, 'What is it? What will it do next? Is it hiding? Is it climbing?' Provide a running commentary on the actions of the child, validating and sometimes interpreting the actions.

Is it a plane . . . ?

Following work on vehicles, pretend that a plastic drink bottle is an aeroplane or a rocket, a speedboat or a hot-air balloon, by making it move in different ways. Give the children some bottles and ask them which vehicles they can make.

Rabbit and fox

Use rabbit and fox puppets and a cardboard box as a home. The rabbit hides in the box when the fox comes. When the fox leaves, the rabbit collects food, but has to hide again when the fox returns. Encourage the children to call out to warn the rabbit. Allow the child to play with the puppets in the same setting so that the narrative is established for them to play within.

Ambush

An adult hides under a sheet and is camouflaged using a cover of paper leaves, real leaves or paper-tissue 'snowflakes'. As courageous volunteers pass by, the creature under the leaves jumps up and chases them away. The sheet and the leaves together make a spectacular sight. Sewing ribbons, beads on strings and metallic plastic strips onto the sheet can provide even greater impact.

Feed the snake

Make a snake from a rolled-up blanket or long sock, sewing on large buttons, inserting small lights, or using circles of sticky paper for eyes. Each child holds a piece of pretend food. Food packaging or plastic fruit can be used for this. Make the snake hiss loudly and stare in a very pronounced way at the food before darting to grab it. The child can either relinquish the food or hide it from the snake's bite. This activity focuses the child's attention towards where the snake's eyes are pointing and on its intention to take the food.

It's there!

Put something that belongs to you, such as a hat, on a table and pretend that you cannot seem to find it, even though it is obvious to everyone where it is. The children attempt to help you find it.

Hot potato

Pass round a real, warm potato. The children must pretend that it is too hot to handle and quickly pass it to someone else. As they become familiar with this narrative, the warm potato can be replaced with a cold potato, then a plastic one, and eventually with an imaginary one. Imaginary potatoes can be as hot as you wish!

Soak me

Play throwing buckets of imaginary water over each other. Give children a real towel to dry off the imaginary water.

Cooks

Use a plastic frying pan to cook pretend food from junk materials such as plastic bottles, cardboard boxes, string, beads, bottle tops and buttons. As the food is handed out on plates, say, for example, 'Mmm . . . who would like some sausages?' and 'Oh, you will need a knife and fork with that.'

Illustrated stories

Take a familiar story that the children have heard many times before. Stories that work well are likely to reflect the experience and culture of the children and may range from traditional fairy tales and folk stories to Disney animations. This will work particularly well if the children have heard several versions of the same story and have also seen it on video or television. Use the familiar story as a starting point for a new story. Use puppets, other toys or objects created from junk materials to represent the important parts of the story, or dramatise them using a few improvised costumes. Use lots of animated expressions to guide the children through the most relevant parts.

Take a sheet

Take a cotton sheet and use it to improvise with the children, taking turns to try out new and creative ideas. Drape the sheet over some tables or chairs and make it into a cave, a tent, a house or a boat. Ask who lives inside and what they are doing. Alternatively, wrap the sheet around your body – perhaps you are a snake, a bear, a bird, a jellyfish, a ghost, an Egyptian mummy or a hospital patient. Waft the sheet in the air – it is the wind; spin it around – it is a hurricane. Hold it up high at each corner – it is a spider's web, a whale's mouth or an ominous fog. Have fun!

'Have fun!'

3 Developing sub-plots within the narrative

For these activities, children should be capable of understanding some language and pretence. In the middle stage, children begin to act on ideas in the same ways that they act upon objects at an earlier stage. In stage 3, this is taken a step further by focusing on how different ideas can relate to the main narrative but be separate from it. The children use language and pretence within extended narratives, rather than focusing on a single or simple idea, and then begin to develop these into more complex and sophisticated forms.

The following activities and teaching structures all work by the teacher creating a scenario in which the narrative can develop. The children are invited to participate individually at first, and as they become more confident, they can be encouraged to work collaboratively on small activities within the main structure.

Shops

The children visit a play shop and buy whatever they wish using pretend money. This might begin with buying toys from a toy shop or toy food from a supermarket. The children should soon be able to improvise, pretending that boxes, bottles, string, beads and so on can be anything that they imagine. Piling up the purchases makes this game more entertaining as the children struggle to carry them back to their chairs.

The children could visit a pretend music shop and pretend to try out the musical instruments before they buy them. Alternatively, they could go to buy a CD of their favourite performer. The shopkeeper can pretend not to know it, so the customer must sing the song to help them find it.

We're all going on a summer holiday

The chairs are pushed together and someone puts on a peaked hat. The driver asks the nearest passenger where they want to go, then sets off, the passengers singing joyfully as the bus travels along. If the children find it difficult to think of a destination, you could offer a choice using postcards, photos or pages from a travel brochure as visual prompts. The destination could be local – for example, the child's house – or it could be a distant or even fantasy location such as the Emerald Palace in *The Wizard of Oz*.

Having arrived at the new destination, the passengers have a short stop to explore the sights and sounds. As in a coach tour, the adult tour guide should give a brief description of the place, highlighting any exciting sights and any hazards to be aware of.

Jungle explorers

Pretend to be in the jungle, where there are lots of dangerous animals to look out for. For each type of animal, a particular action could be required. For example, there might be tigers – if you hear a growling noise you must stand very still until the tiger passes by. There might be scary spiders that jump on you from passing trees – if you find any you must catch them and put them in a spider bag. There might also be crocodiles that will bite your legs – if you see one you must hop from foot to foot, so they do not know which foot to bite first.

Doctor, doctor!

A child pretends to be injured. Invite one of the group to be the doctor and encourage the others to help: 'The doctor needs someone to hold up the patient's arm', 'The doctor needs you to give the patient this medicine', 'The doctor wants an ambulance', 'Can you all help carry the stretcher to the ambulance?'

> In one drama lesson while opening a window, I was about to pretend to be dramatically swept across the floor by a hurricane that had blown in. Unfortunately, my finger got trapped in the window and I fell to the floor. Bleeding profusely, I called for an ambulance. Believing I was still pretending, the whole class jumped on me, gave me injections and medicine and wrapped me in every bandage they could find!

At the seaside

Pretend to be at the seaside. Would you like an ice cream? Which flavour would you like? Would you prefer strawberry or vanilla? (Or, would you prefer strawberry or slug-slime?!) Who would like a bucket and spade? Can you make imaginary sandcastles? Come on! Let's jump in the sea and splash in the waves. Oh, look out to sea . . . What is it? What is coming towards us? Take the children's suggestions and write them into the developing narrative.

Adult in role

The adult takes on the role of a character that will be familiar to all the children. This might be someone from a film, such as one of the *Harry Potter* series, from a story, such as Goldilocks, or a figure such as Santa Claus from general culture. Use the ideas that surround the character to explore familiar but meaningful issues using language. For example, Santa Claus might say, 'Ho, ho, ho, Merry Christmas, everyone. Oh no, I have lost all my presents! Could you help me look for them? Look under the chair . . . they're not there. Oh dear, thank you for looking. Perhaps you could help me by looking for them in the cupboard. Oh, they are not there either. Who else can help me look? Oh good, let's all go and look around the room.' After everyone has pretended to look, he might say, 'Oh dear, come and sit with me, children. I'm sorry, I don't know what I have done with the presents. [To one child] What did you want for Christmas? Yes, that is a good present.' Santa writes the answer down, asks the other children and lists their answers. Then he can ask them how we can make some new presents. After listening to the answers, he might say, 'Which of these boxes, bags and bottles could we use to make that present? Yes, that is a good idea. I will use my Santa magic to turn it into your present. Now, which present was next on my list? Here you are, children – here are your presents. Merry Christmas!'

Aliens

The children draw a picture of the strangest alien creature they can imagine. They give it a name and an unusual characteristic. You might prepare a list of characteristics for children who have difficulty in generating their own. Make time before the game to discuss how this creature might behave towards strangers, what they like and dislike, whether they would be able to communicate with others and, if so, what type of voice they would have. The children sit in different places around the room, holding their pictures. You then play an character rather like Alice in the alternative looking-glass world. As you encounter each creature, you attempt to find out a little about them and how they might return to their own planet. Each child must answer the questions as if they were the alien creature. You are supporting and extending both language and pretence while encouraging the child to maintain their character in role.

Animal Farm

This narrative is based around *Farmer Duck* by Martin Waddell or *Animal Farm* by George Orwell, depending on the age and ability of the children. The activity could follow work on these books or be used to introduce or explore some of the ideas in them. The children play the roles of overworked animals who take control of their farm. In role as the farmer, find out how each animal feels and what they think about their work: 'Why will you not work more quickly, little duck? Are you sitting down again? What is the matter with you? So you are sad? And you are crying? Perhaps you are bored and you want some more work to do . . . hmm?' Ask the other animals about their work and whether they like the tasks they have to do. Then announce, 'You think that you could manage this farm without me – well, let me see you try. Here is a spade and here are the keys for my tractor. I am going on holiday and when I return I shall find out what good farmers you really are.' The animals must now organise themselves to do the work, using the list of daily jobs you have left. Out of role, you now assist the children to discuss the jobs and who will do them. Ask them what the farmer will think if they do not complete all the jobs before they return. Will the farmer be angry or sad? Does the farmer think that you will make a good job of sweeping the yard? Will they sack all the animals and send them to work elsewhere? Will the animals take over the farm, like in the story, or will something else happen?

Chapter 6
Supporting work and positive behaviour

For many children on the autism spectrum, school work is a positive experience. Its structured content and reliance on rules and routines provide a learning environment that they find predictable and sometimes stimulating. This chapter describes how learning can be enhanced through classroom and time management, and through the careful use of structure to help each child to understand what is required of them.

Children on the autism spectrum have a very different thinking style from their peers, and this may result in some different preferences. They may focus on completely different aspects of a subject, and this may lead them to misunderstand its underlying features.

Case study

Harry was an 8-year-old boy whose current fascination was the subject of death. On discovering that most serious car accidents occurred to passengers who were wearing seat belts, he decided not to travel in vehicles if he had to wear one. This developed to the point that he insisted on having the seat belts removed from his parents' car. He was worried that simply having them in the car increased the risk of such an accident. Eventually, Harry was persuaded by his parents that statistics showed no increased probability of having a serious car accident when the passengers wore a St Christopher medal and a seat belt – and Harry reluctantly agreed to wear both.

What the child on the autism spectrum takes from a lesson may be very different from the teacher's expectations. You should never assume that because the child has completed their work, they have understood in the same way as other children. This may not be the case, and the child may be building their understanding on very wobbly foundations. It is therefore important to monitor the child's experience closely and to check thoroughly their understanding of the work to ensure they have the necessary skills and knowledge to build on in the next lesson.

Individual programmes or plans
Assessment and IEPs
Assumptions should not be made about the abilities of children on the autistic spectrum. They often have high-level skills that are unsupported by other areas of understanding, typically areas of social understanding and communication. Deficiency in understanding in these areas has a pervasive effect on the learning in all areas, but it is common for children with autism spectrum conditions to mask their poor understanding by learning how to behave in particular circumstances. It is therefore necessary for a specialist teacher or psychologist to carry out a proper assessment of these children so that fragmented learning is not compounded at a later stage.

Each child on the autism spectrum requires an individual education programme (IEP) that identifies the focus of the child's education over several weeks or months. It should centre on the child's needs (rather than what the teacher is teaching) and should frequently refer to areas of difficulty such as social understanding, social skills, communication, play and creativity.

An IEP should interpret how difficulties present themselves and how the child can help themselves to develop skills in these areas. Targets should be concise enough to be measurable, but broad enough to allow for genuine learning – rather than learning to perform the next step or to 'jump through hoops'. Targets may be phrased to allow the freedom to follow a learning adventure, while providing a focus to the direction of this journey. The targets should then be discussed and strategies developed that might lead the child towards that target. Strategies should be constantly evaluated and re-evaluated to ensure the best fit for the child as they respond to the activities.

An IEP should also reflect the child's strengths, and specify how these will be integrated into the wider curriculum. Strengths should be used to help the child develop skills and understanding, especially in areas where they have particular difficulty. A strength in drawing, for example, could be used to help the child develop their language skills, if the activity is structured carefully to build up the use of meaningful verbal labels for the child's drawings. Building on strengths has the added benefit of developing self-esteem and skills that can be used in work later on in life.

The IEP should be discussed with parents and all school staff. If the child is to maximise their progress in these difficult areas of understanding, they will require as much support as possible.

Weekly plans

While IEPs are useful for setting the main aims, the plan should be broken down into smaller targets for weekly and daily use. Like the IEP, the weekly plan should take account of strengths and weaknesses.

Here are some sample weekly targets for John, a 6-year-old boy with autism in a mainstream classroom:

- John should speak to the other boys on his table when they ask him a question. To start with, the children should ask questions about a favourite toy. (John can speak, but chooses not to speak to the other boys.)

- John should use his 'No, thank you' symbol card when he does not want to do something. He has become very anxious and sometimes angry when he has been asked to go to the playground. The cards are intended to give him an alternative rejection strategy. However, he is allowed to reject a maximum of two items each day.

- John should complete a comprehension worksheet after his reading each morning to check his understanding of the story. (John appears to read the words on the page competently but may not understand what these words mean, either individually or when they are put together.)

○ John should join in the play-drama games, in which he must respond, not to the teacher, but to another child. (John likes some of the play-drama games we have done in the past, but he constantly refers to the teacher and excludes the other children. This target attempts to re-direct his attention towards his peers.)

It is usually a good idea to teach a new skill or concept in very small steps. This helps to ensure that the child has understood or remembered all the component parts. A 5-year-old child with autism impressed his teachers and his family by learning all his times tables. He could effortlessly answer questions such as, 'What is three times seven?' It was not until later that they discovered that he had used his remarkable memory for songs to remember each individual numeric fact and had no understanding of the mathematical concepts involved. He was therefore unable to apply the skill to answer questions such as 'If three bags have seven apples each, how many apples are there altogether?'

The National Curriculum

In the UK, almost all children work on curricula that refer to the National Curriculum guidelines. These may need only minor modifications to fit the needs of more able children on the autism spectrum. For children who have greater difficulties in learning, the National Curriculum will need substantial modification. These children need a curriculum that is meaningful, relevant to their experience and to their needs, broad and balanced, and that connects them with others so that they learn through a shared understanding of the experience.

It is important that if the National Curriculum is modified to such an extent, you do not lose sight of the needs of the child. To teach only National Curriculum content, knowledge and skills without reference to the child's needs is to neglect their entitlement to a balanced and relevant curriculum. Ensuring that the needs of the child remain paramount and central to the curriculum they are offered is a time-consuming task that should not be underestimated. Such modification does not mean that the child with autism should not be taught alongside their peers in a mainstream classroom. Neither does it mean that the child with autism should be taught on the periphery of the room by a teaching assistant. Rather, the child and their needs and abilities should be brought into the heart of the class so that their special interests can be shared and made meaningful by the whole class. Additionally, all the children in the class can benefit from the depth of planning, detailed observation, assessment and evaluation that is required for the child with autism.

'The child and their needs and abilities should be brought into the heart of the class.'

Many of the activities described in this book can be linked to the National Curriculum, and may provide foundations for the successful study of the subjects at some stage in the future. Some examples are given opposite.

Case study

John and another child made an alien monster using construction materials and a visual plan. John took turns in placing the materials together, and did not attempt to dominate the work. (Design and Technology)

Mythily used her 'No, thank you' symbol card when she did not want to do something. (English: speaking and listening)

Noula found PE meaningless and refused to join in any team event. She was reluctant even to get changed before the lesson. The teacher found quite by accident that Noula was willing to hold a stick with a long yellow ribbon hanging from it. She liked to spin around holding this stick so that the ribbon spiralled around her. The teacher introduced some suitable music and a stage light and made it into a dance lesson. All the other children were allowed to copy the movements that Noula used in her dance. Noula's attitude towards PE improved once she was allowed to have 5 minutes' dancing at the end of the lesson. (PE)

Eleni became fascinated by the Egyptian mummies that her teacher introduced in history. Eleni had not shown any interest in the subject up to this point. A life-size mummy was made by the children and displayed in the corner of the classroom. The teacher then introduced the rest of the topic on Ancient Egypt from the perspective of the mummy. This sometimes took the form of asking Eleni, for example, 'What did the mummy see the pharaoh do to the slave?' Eleni showed remarkable concentration on these lessons for as long as the mummy was in the room. (History)

Thanasis liked to count any objects that he found. Walking down the school corridors always took him much longer than the other children because he would be silently counting pictures on the wall displays or the number of blue tiles on the floor. Thanasis was making slow progress in his Spanish lessons, until his teacher started organising the work so that each activity involved some aspect of counting. (Modern Foreign Languages)

Strategies for classroom management
Organisation of furniture and equipment
Children can be given additional help in understanding what is expected of them by allocating different parts of the home, classroom or school to different types of activity: food is consumed in one area but not in another, painting is done on this table but not on that one, we sit in a circle in this part of the classroom but in that part we sit in pairs at small tables. Using the furniture to create small individual work places, art and technology areas, play areas and quiet reading corners helps the children to distinguish the different types of behaviour required for different types of work.

For children who are easily distracted, the physical organisation of the room can be used to compartmentalise the available space. A child who is easily annoyed by other children, or who frequently annoys them, might be better completing individual work on the other side of the cupboard or facing towards the wall than facing other children.

Working independently and in groups
Some children on the autism spectrum do not cope with following rules that they do not find meaningful, and prefer to follow their own agenda. These children are conspicuous in a classroom because they choose to work or play independently from the class. Using this preference can be an effective strategy if the classroom and the curriculum allow time and space to do this. Such a

learning environment would allow the child to work independently when they are positively engaged in their learning. For example, a child might prefer to spend long periods of time working on the computer, in which case you could organise work to be completed in this way. Another child might benefit from having some dedicated space in the classroom to draw pictures whenever they need to. Children on the autism spectrum would also have a programme of work that would help them develop a balanced and functional understanding of the world. So if the child were spending periods working alone, you would ensure that there were activities during the day that involved them in meaningful group work in which their skills and strengths were used. In this way, the work in which the child has succeeded independently can be generalised into a group situation: the child learns to apply their skills in a social setting and understands that their ideas are meaningful to others.

With children on the autism spectrum, it is important to develop both the areas of strength and the areas of need. The work on developing areas that the child finds difficult and that pose an obstacle to their learning should be tackled by using the child's interests and experience to help them, so that they learn to focus on the essentials of social communication. This can be done through designing individual programmes or plans.

Visual organisation

In many children on the autism spectrum, the sense of sight is particularly dominant. Organisational cards can be used as visual reminders to let children know what they are expected to do and to remain focused on a task. These cards are similar to the communication cards described in Chapter 4, consisting of laminated photos and symbols displayed in a specified place in the home or classroom. For example:

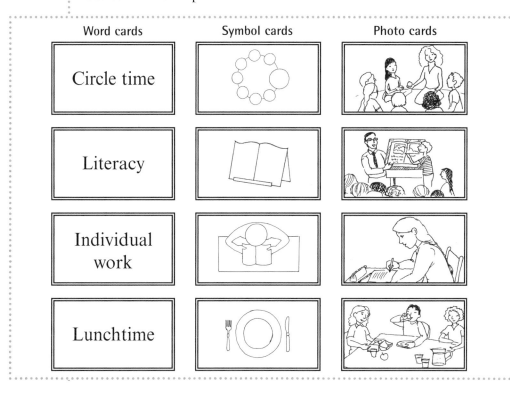

The illustration opposite shows photos, symbols and written word cards. The choice about which to use is dictated by the ease with which they are used in practice. For less able or very young children, objects can be used to show what is coming next or the equipment they need to collect. For older and more able pupils, written words can be used to provide a 'jobs to do' list. A diary or student planner can be used to help pupils remember the sequences of the day.

Organisational cards can be displayed near the front of a class or near where children are seated in groups, so they can be referred to as needed. Cards can be displayed by a child's desk or small-group work area, or kept in a box or folder that is stored with the activity itself.

As each part of the sequence is completed, the child or adult can remove it from the display and refer to the next card. This helps the children understand what they are expected to do next and when all the tasks will be finished. Activities that are enjoyed by the child should be included somewhere in the organisational sequence. These may be interspersed with other tasks or left as a reward until the others are completed to the teacher's satisfaction.

"Does anyone know the answer?"

I wish he would ask me sometimes and not that boy called "anyone".

Organisational cards can be used to structure a period as long as a whole day or part of it, or as short as the next few minutes. The use of organisational cards should be dictated by the needs of the children. If a child is having particular difficulty in remembering how to complete a sequential task, the cards can be used to guide them. These card systems may also be useful in providing all children in inclusive settings with visual information about the structure of the day, what work they are expected to do and where to go to complete the work.

Explicit instructions

Children on the autism spectrum often make literal interpretations of speech, even if the interpretation breaks their normal expectations. Using humour, and particularly sarcasm, with children who have autism spectrum conditions can be difficult owing to this over-literality, and it should be done with care. Even asking questions can be hampered by over-literality. Questions such as 'Have you got a pen?' (meaning 'Have you got a pen that I could borrow?') and 'Could you lend me a pen?' could be answered by the child saying 'Yes' but not handing over a pen. This type of response could be seen as cheeky, but usually the child is simply concentrating on a literal interpretation of the words without giving any consideration to what the speaker actually meant by them. As these children often have difficulty in understanding the subtleties of language and cannot easily read between the lines, requests, guidance and instructions should be given explicitly. The use of clear and unambiguous statements can be of great help in communicating with children on the autism spectrum. (See Chapter 7 for more on this.)

For children who have low levels of verbal language, explicit directions can be given non-verbally. Hand and arm signals can show, for example, where the children should go and when they should stop doing something. Organisational cards or objects can also be used to give directions. All staff need to be consistent in the use of signals.

Routines

You can use the children's liking of familiar routines to help them feel comfortable with what is going to happen during the day. Routines also help the children to understand why things are happening and to cope with small changes to the day.

Although routines can be very effective, they are a double-edged sword. The constant danger in teaching and supporting children with autism is that they will become over-reliant on routines and rituals and not take proper consideration of the new information that is introduced. Flexibility within routines and organisational cards is needed to prevent the children from becoming rigid in their use of familiar routines. This flexibility should be built into teaching programmes.

Avoiding anxiety triggers

The perceptual world of children with autism spectrum conditions can be very different from that experienced by you or by normally developing children, and their communication difficulties compound the problem. When something happens that causes the child to be irritated, anxious, angry, content or extremely happy, it is often not clear to others what the trigger was.

Difficulties can be caused by almost any type of change – a new routine at home or school, the local supermarket changing the position of their video display, physiological changes in the child's body, a different type of fabric conditioner that leaves a different smell on the child's clothes, or an elder sister who starts wearing earrings. If the child does not communicate the problem to those who can help with it, the problem can become compounded and entrenched. To take the supermarket video display example, the child may refuse to go to any shops because their original problem has not been resolved. Or they may go to the supermarket but insist on dismantling the new display because they believe it to be in the wrong place.

Children who are anxious, frustrated or angry, or who expect to be upset by the events of the day are unlikely to learn effectively. The best solution to these problems lies in close and constant observation and an in-depth knowledge of the child. While the problem may be huge in the mind of the child, they may not realise that this needs to be communicated to others before other people will also have it in their minds. The child therefore needs to learn how to communicate about the things that trouble them.

Expectations of behaviour

It is important that the children on the autism spectrum learn to respond to consistent expectations of their work and behaviour. All staff should attempt to maintain consistency in the eyes of the children and deal firmly but gently with any transgressions from these expectations. In designing a new activity or programme, the teacher should consider the implications in the longer term and whether it will create new behaviours that will have to be unlearnt at some stage in the future. For example, when Joseph learned about pregnancy, it took him years to learn not to ask every large person that he met whether they were going to have a baby.

Tolerance and valuing of difference

Many teaching staff find great difficulty in accepting the behaviour of children on the autistic spectrum. The child who scribbles on the cover of their book is thought not to be listening, and the child who loudly complains that they are bored in class is thought to be disruptive rather than honest. It is important that everyone learns to be tolerant of differences in others, even if these are difficult to understand at the time. And, ideally, you should not only be tolerant of the differences that are so evident in autism, but positively value these differences. Children on the autism spectrum can often bring a novel perspective to teaching and learning that can enhance the experience for all involved. Some have special skills that are far above the level of most other children and that can be genuinely admired. Others on the autistic spectrum face a far greater learning challenge than their peers and make slower progress, but gain hugely from being with them. For some, the tiniest of steps can be a gigantic leap into the unknown; such steps should be celebrated for the achievements that they are.

Unstructured time

In some ways, subject teaching is only the tip of the iceberg when educating children on the autism spectrum, as only a small part of their educational needs is met in this way. For many of these children, the routines of regular work make them feel comfortable; they like knowing what they should be doing. Conversely, the times that provide most difficulty are break times and relatively unstructured lesson time. Asking a child with autism to play until the end of the lesson, or to collaborate with another child, or to enjoy a free choice and movement time, can be very difficult for them to cope with. Some children will need clear instructions about what they should be doing at such times. Other children need to be taught explicitly how to play in the playground or how to collaborate on a joint task.

Here are a few suggestions to help children on the autistic spectrum in these situations.

Unstructured classroom times

- Ensure the child on the autism spectrum understands what they should be doing, and what to do if they become confused or uninterested. You might give them a list of activities that should be either completed or attempted before the end of the lesson.
- Encourage children who struggle with unstructured time to cope with small choices, one at a time, so that they become less dependent on the teacher providing the structure.
- Allow the child the opportunity to work away from noise or other children moving around in unstructured parts of the lesson.
- Sometimes unstructured times in lessons allow the child the freedom to work at length on something that interests them and are an effective way of learning.

Break time

- ○ Give the child a clearly defined job to do, such as handing out footballs or delivering merit cards from the teacher to the other children for good playing.
- ○ Find other children who will listen to the child with autism talk about their interests. Can these children be encouraged to play together?
- ○ Organise a break-time club for children who have similar interests to the child with autism, such as a computer, reading or gardening club.
- ○ Teach the child a useful skill that will enable them to play a part in break-time activities. They could, for example, learn how to be a good goalkeeper so that they become a valued member of the lunch-break football game.

Motivation and reward

'Different children will respond to different types of reward.'

Children on the autism spectrum need to understand when they have been successful. The social praise that is used with normally developing children may be insufficient or unwelcome. Or they may simply be indifferent to it. Different children will respond to different types of reward. For example, they might respond to:

- ○ a reward system, such as awarding points or stickers, or simply ticking the child's work;
- ○ earning time on the school computer;
- ○ praising by using a particular word or sound that the child enjoys;
- ○ being allowed to engage in a favourite activity – for some individuals, choosing from a selection of toy animals and lining these up on the radiator cover may motivate them to complete task after task.

Sometimes the motivation is intrinsic to the activity, and therefore an extrinsic reward is not required – this is an especially valuable form of motivation. Many of the activities described in Chapters 3–5 are designed to elicit these feelings in children with autism. This is particularly important because children on the autism spectrum are often the ones who find these areas of functioning to be the least motivating and consequently do not learn effectively from them.

Making generalisations

Children with autism tend to be relatively rigid thinkers and will sometimes have problems in transferring the skills or the knowledge that they learn in one situation to another. For some, a different teacher, a new classroom or the use of different materials can create huge difficulty in knowing how to proceed with something that they are quite used to doing. Even seeing the teacher with a change of hairstyle or clothing may disorient a child, and they have to adjust to the person's new appearance before they can relate to them again.

Children with autism may therefore need to be taught the same skills or knowledge several times in different places with different people and with different materials. This should be carefully planned into the teaching programmes of children who have had clear difficulties with generalisation, and should be considered for all children on the autism spectrum.

The most important strategy

Although books such as this one offer effective strategies for teaching children with autism spectrum conditions, they do not replace the most basic requisite – people. There is no substitute for them. Children with autism need other people to structure, guide, celebrate and share the experience of learning. Children on the autism spectrum need caring, sensitive and persistent people, just as children with a visual impairment need spectacles and a child with paraplegia needs a wheelchair.

Simply paying attention to the learning of a child with autism is perhaps the most important strategy in this book. Engage with the children and allow them to learn with you. Staff ratios suitable for children on the autism spectrum are, of necessity, high. This is not because the behaviour of these children is particularly difficult to integrate into a normal classroom. It is because their education requires sensitive, persistent and creative teachers, parents and other professionals who value the child or children with autism and want to engage with them.

Chapter 7
Supporting everyone involved

Teachers with a child on the autism spectrum in their class have an additional responsibility. Not only are they concerned with the education of the child, but they also have a responsibility towards that child's family. Children on the autism spectrum present challenges to those who live and work with them, and these challenges are best met by those who know the child well working together. The parents, siblings, teachers, teaching assistants, supervisory assistants, therapists and other children all need support to help them meet these challenges – and the best form of support is that which all of these people can give to each other.

Mutual support is particularly important when the people involved with the child with autism are relatively isolated from each other. Many families and people that teach children with autism have moments of despair and feel that no one else really understands their child or children. It is therefore all the more vital that ways are found for these people to work together to support each other and the child.

Supporting families

Critical to the successful education of a child with autism is the interface between the school and the home. Parents usually value teachers sharing information about the child's work, relationships, interests and problems. Finding time for this can seem difficult, but just a brief telephone call or note home can often provide the important bit of information that the family want. Similarly, information from home can be really useful in understanding the child's behaviour or in providing a vital clue for moving forward in their educational programme. Because children on the autism spectrum have communication difficulties, they cannot be relied on to convey relevant information between home and school. A note in the home–school diary can provide a helpful prompt for some children, who are then able to talk about the issue.

What parents want

Parents don't want or expect teachers to know all the answers or to be super-heroes or heroines. In fact, if this is how teachers are seen, it may undermine a parent's confidence and their ability to manage on difficult days. Neither, however, do parents want teachers to throw their hands in the air despairingly and exclaim that the child cannot manage in the class. What parents usually want is a shared dialogue about their child's education and how that relates to other aspects of their life.

Sometimes families have particular problems that are evident at home but not at school or in other environments. In this case, it is helpful for the teacher or teaching assistant who knows the child well to work with the family on finding out why these problems occur and finding solutions to them. This can be time consuming, but it is sometimes the most valuable contribution that can be made to the child's ability to learn and live a happy and productive life. Some schools are creative in allowing their staff time for this, and many teachers commit considerable amounts of time to working with families.

Case study

Jane was a teacher of a Year-1 class in a mainstream school. One of her pupils, Jamie, was on the autism spectrum. He was able to follow the daily routines in the school but needed help to play at break times, as he would otherwise sit quietly in the corner of the field. At home, Jamie was very different. He spent much of his time insisting on having his mother's sole attention. If anyone else – even his father – came into the room, Jamie would find ways of causing such a commotion that normal family life was completely disrupted. After several years of this, Jamie's family had learnt to make sure that Jamie's desire for undivided attention was a priority. Unfortunately, things had recently worsened. One of Jamie's new behaviours included insisting that no television was permitted after 6 pm.

Jamie's teacher Jane started working more closely with Jamie's family, looking at the reasons why he might be doing this. They were amazed by reports of his conformity and passivity at school; how he would sit through the Big Book stories in Literacy, quietly eat his lunch with the other children, and was starting to form a friendship with a slightly older girl from the next class. At Jane's invitation, Jamie's parents decided to visit school without his knowing. They saw, from a distance, their son sitting in class, following instructions and working alongside others. They were so pleased with his behaviour that at playtime they decided to praise him, and walked on to the playground. Jamie shot them a glance and then turned away as if they were not there. Jamie's parents had never seen this type of behaviour before and took it very personally.

After several weeks they contacted the school to talk to Jane. She agreed to visit them and Jamie at home. When she arrived, Jamie ignored her as he had his parents. In discussing this, Jane and Jamie's parents both started to feel that they had learnt a bit more about Jamie and how he thought about other people. They also discovered that when his teacher was in the house, Jamie did not use any of his attention-grabbing behaviour and sat quietly, playing a video game. Over the following weeks, Jane and Jamie's parents worked together and gave Jamie ways of structuring his time at home, offering activities that he enjoyed doing with people in the house other than his mother. The tensions that were building in the family started to reduce.

Some schools have been effective as community resources, providing a centre for the people in the local community to socialise as well as to learn together. This can give children on the autism spectrum – as well as their parents, brothers and sisters – an opportunity to be part of something bigger. It can provide an opportunity to talk and share experience and to learn and grow together. For children who are in specialised settings and go to school away from their peers, this is particularly important.

Supporting professionals

Teachers and teaching assistants also need support in their work. Teaching children on the autism spectrum can be very draining emotionally, and some children make additional physical and mental demands. Having the opportunity to discuss the successes and challenges of teaching these children can be helpful in coping with these demands. It is important that the school recognises the problems and provides opportunities for staff to talk about their work. In many areas of the country there are support groups for professionals (and parents). There are also Internet support groups and professional courses that provide the opportunity to talk with other people who have personal experience and an understanding of autism (see Resources).

This chapter suggests some games and activities that are designed to help people who have a mutual interest in autism explore some ideas together. These can be used as part of a training day or simply by colleagues working together to develop their understanding of autism.

Food for thought
When everything is working well and the child makes a small step forward which transforms their life from that moment on, teaching children with autism can be one of the most exhilarating professions available.

Off-the-shelf approaches and strategies are rarely sufficient in themselves and will frequently break down in practice. The role of the experienced and knowledgeable professional is to understand the child as a person, and the autism spectrum as a learning style – and then to solve difficulties that the child has in developing their learning.

The following exercises are designed to help develop a better understanding of autism and autism spectrum conditions, and extend your ability to work out possible solutions to difficulties often encountered by children on the autism spectrum.

Confused narratives
The activity opposite, based on the café scenario in Chapter 1, is designed to simulate the sense of disengagement experienced by people on the autism spectrum. Invite participants to pair up. Give each pair a photocopy of the scripts on pages 7–8, and invite them to read Version 1, then Version 2, as role plays. Then get into small groups to answer the questions.

Inclusion
Inclusive education can be a wonderful opportunity or a living nightmare for children on the autism spectrum. Where inclusion is successful, a significant part is played by the school and the professionals working there. Inclusion is not allocating a place to a child in a mainstream classroom, but finding ways to make the experience of the child on the autism spectrum socially and academically relevant. This may mean wrapping the curriculum around the child, so that the relevance is apparent throughout the day, and so that it affords meaningful opportunities for the child to engage successfully with others.
The *Inclusion* exercise on page 60 is designed to help these professionals think through how they might make a significant difference to a child on the autism spectrum who is about to join a mainstream class.

Confused narratives

Questions

1. Describe how you felt after acting in these two scenarios.

2. How could the two customers in version 2 have found common ground, given that they were each determined to follow their own concerns?

3. Write a script for a third scenario as follows:

   Customer 1 insists on sitting in the window seat because they would not feel comfortable eating elsewhere. Customer 2 is an irate parent with three small children. The café owner is fastidious about cleanliness but uninterested in the needs of customers. He dislikes working in the café and really wants to be at home watching the football match.

4. Re-write the script so that all the characters are able to engage within a shared narrative in which they pay regard to individual needs and interests.

5. Now think about a child with autism whom you know. Discuss with someone else how the child's own way of seeing everyday interaction and communication differs from the commonly accepted view of the world.

Inclusion

Rupert is an 8-year-old boy who has recently moved to your school. His family used to live on a farm but have moved into town. Rupert is having difficulty settling into a new home and lifestyle, and into a new school. He is a rigid thinker and likes to follow rules and fit into routines. He is capable of completing much of the written work required of his year group but is very reluctant to write more than is absolutely necessary. He is also reluctant to give more than one-word answers to spoken questions, unless the subject is one that he is interested in. He does not feel comfortable in the playground at break times and can usually be found walking around the perimeter of the school field on his own. Rupert does like watching television and playing computer games. He will sometimes mention the animals on the farm where he lived.

Discuss the following questions. For any that you find difficult, discuss how you might go about finding an answer. Think about how you could check to see if your ideas are working in practice.

1. How might Rupert feel better included in a Literacy lesson? How might the organisation of time in Literacy be used to help him cope with extended writing tasks?

2. Rupert feels lonely in the playground and does not attempt to join in the games with the other children. How might his interest in television and computers be used to help other children play with him?

3. The children are working on a project about the differences between rural and urban life. How might Rupert take a central role in helping the other children understand these differences and organise their collective work for a display?

4. How might Rupert be encouraged to talk in group discussion and question-and-answer sessions? How might he be encouraged to initiate conversation with others?

5. How can the organisation of the day be made clear for Rupert's benefit? Are there any benefits for the teaching staff and other children in this?

6. What role could Rupert's parents have in helping him settle into his new school? How might they be invited to do this?

"I'm looking for a finished piece of work and a quiet classroom by lunchtime."

bec

Simple language

For children with autism in the early stages of language development, instructions and requests should be kept simple. The exercise *Keep it Simple* on page 62 is designed to heighten awareness of the complexity of some of the language we use, and how it could be simplified.

Over-literality

Children on the autism spectrum often have difficulty in understanding ambiguous statements. The *Keep it Unambiguous* exercise on page 62 is designed to heighten awareness of the ambiguity in everyday language and how it could be avoided.

Levels of interest

Children on the autism spectrum are often attracted to objects or particular features of objects not normally of interest to other children of their age or ability. One child, for example, found anything spinning particularly attractive. A visit to the shops caused problems because he wanted to watch the ceiling fan in one shop and refused to leave. Another child, who was fascinated by the colour blue, was asked his opinion of a painting upon returning from a trip to the local art gallery. He could not remember the painting, but had a detailed memory of the blue tiles on the floor that nobody else had noticed. These perceptions become part of the child's experience and form the building blocks of their understanding. This behaviour is not specific to autism, of course; everyone prioritises some interests over others. In many children on the autism spectrum, however, the priorities are unusual and need to be recognised.

Recognising how the child would prioritise their interests will help you to avoid problems and to teach more effectively. If an activity is focused on an interest that is too strong, it will dominate the child's attention and obstruct their ability to consider other aspects of the experience. Conversely, activities that are unstimulating will not draw the child's attention to the opportunities being offered. In this situation, the child may resort to using self-stimulatory, repetitive behaviours that have a higher-interest value.

It can be helpful to make a list of a child's interests by careful observation of them in different settings. The list on page 63 can be used or adapted to help identify those interests. If this list is not at all relevant to the particular child, make your own list, and make it as detailed as you can. When it is complete, re-order it so that the items are in order of the child's interest.

Use of language

Keep it simple

The following statements are unnecessarily complex. Re-write them into their simplest form without losing the essential meaning. All can be reduced to two or three words.

▶ I would like you to complete this worksheet by writing all your answers in the boxes.

▶ Please come here, I would like to talk to you about that incident.

▶ No, it is not fair as you had a turn yesterday and it is someone else's turn today. Rashid, you can come here and have a go.

▶ In this class, we don't behave like that; we don't wave our hands in the air trying to get attention.

▶ I would like you all to look in this direction when I am speaking to you.

▶ You have done incredibly well with that piece of work. Your teacher and your parents will be very pleased with you – well done!

Keep it unambiguous

Look at the list of questions and statements below. They are written so that they could be understood in more than one way. Re-write them so that they are unambiguous and explicit.

▶ Can you pass Sunil the glue?

▶ What is the correct time?

▶ Maria, please don't do that.

▶ When you have finished the last question, you can go.

▶ If you want to go to the toilet, you must put your hand up.

▶ All PE shorts should have your names in them.

▶ The museum holds a collection of ancient mummies.

▶ Who knows the answer?

Interest checklist

Give each area a score as follows:

0 = repulsive or off-putting
1 = complete uninterest
2 = tolerates it
3 = likes it

4 = will request it
5 = will complain if it is removed
6 = will refuse to do anything else if it is in the room

Additional lines are provided for other items of particular interest. These should be significant things in the child's life.

Child's name:

Areas	0–6	Description of child's response
Spinning and revolving objects		
Vehicles		
Animals		
Foods		
Actions and movements		
Action heroes		
Maps		
Timetables		
Sequences – rote counting, timelines		
People		
Loud sounds		
Music		
Vocal sounds		
Video and computers		
Mirrors and shiny objects		
Bright lights and colours		
Teasing		
Building and balancing		
Numbers, letters and written words		
A specific object		
Lining things up		
Putting things in objects		
Collecting things		
Smelling or touching things		
Scary things		
Notes:		

Resources

References

DfES (2002) *Autistic Spectrum Disorders: Good Practice Guidance.* DfES

Jones, G. (2002) *Educational Provision for Children with Autism and Asperger Syndrome.* David Fulton

Sherratt, D. and Donald, G. (2004) 'Connectedness: a shared construction of affect and cognition in children with autism', *British Journal of Special Education.* Vol. 31/1

Sherratt, D. and Peter, M. (2002) *The Development of Play and Drama in Children with Autistic Spectrum Disorders.* David Fulton

Wing, L. (1996) *The Autistic Spectrum: a Guide for Parents and Professionals.* Constable

Further reading

Autism and autism spectrum conditions

Bruner, J. and Feldman, C. (1993) 'Theories of mind and the problem of autism' in S. Baron-Cohen, H. Tager-Flusberg and D. J. Cohen (eds.) *Understanding Other Minds: Perspectives from Autism.* Oxford University Press

Hobson, P. R. (2002) *The Cradle of Thought.* Macmillan

Jordan, R. R. and Powell, S. D. (1995) *Understanding and Teaching Children with Autism.* John Wiley and Sons

Play and drama

Grove, N. and Park, K. (2001) *Developing Social Cognition through Literature and Drama.* Jessica Kingsley

Sherratt, D. (2002) 'Developing pretend play in children with autism: a case study', *Autism: The International Journal of Research and Practice.* Vol. 6/2

Websites

The National Autistic Society
www.nas.org.uk

Treatment and Education of Autistic and Related Communication Handicapped Children
www.teacch.com

Page of interesting information on autism with many links to other autism-related sites
www.isn.net/~jypsy

The Intensive Interaction approach to teaching children on the autism spectrum
www.intensiveinteraction.co.uk

Courses

Birmingham University organises courses for professionals who teach or care for children or adults who have an autism spectrum disorder. These are available by paper-based distance education (with study weekends and regional tutorials); they also have a children's programme available on campus. Courses may be taken by students not based in the UK, providing suitable support arrangements can be made.
www.bham.ac.uk